America's Got Talent Winner

Landau Eugene Murphy, Jr

From Washing Cars to Hollywood Star

Landau Eugene Murphy, Jr.

with Rick Robinson

Headline Books, Inc.
Terra Alta, WV

America's Got Talent Winner Landau Eugene Murphy Jr: From Wshing Cars to Hollywood Star

by Landau Eugene Murphy Jr. with Rick Robinson

copyright ©2014 Landau Eugene Murphy Jr.

To order additional copies of this book or
for book publishing information contact:

Headline Books, Inc.
P.O. Box 52
Terra Alta, WV 26764
www.HeadlineBooks.com

Tel: 800-570-5951
Email: MyBook@HeadlineBooks.com

Art Director, Ashley Teets
Photo contributions by Sterling Snyder

To contact the author:
Burke Allen, Allen Media Strategies
Washington, DC
(703) 589-8960 phone
www.AllenMediaStrategies.com
www.LandauMurphyJr.com

ISBN-13: 978-0-938467-67-0

Library of Congress Number: 2013938676

Landau / by Landau Eugene Murphy Jr with Rick Robinson
        p. cm.
ISBN 978-0938467-67-0
1. Memoir-non-fiction. 2. Music- non-fiction.

PRINTED IN THE UNITED STATES OF AMERICA

To the people from the great state of West Virginia
(and especially the citizens of Logan)

"The show really is about people realizing a dream. And it doesn't get better than a winner like Landau, because he had this dream and he couldn't get a break. He was homeless, he ended up washing cars, he couldn't get a break and he got one on the show and he won. He took his chance, and look at him now. He's a million dollar act in Vegas. It's the stuff of dreams."

— Piers Morgan, judge *on America's Got Talent*

Introduction

by Rick Robinson

Tonight I became a part of the whirlwind known as "Team Landau."

When my publisher, Cathy Teets, called me to see if I would be interested in helping the season six winner of *America's Got Talent*, Landau Eugene Murphy, Jr., put his life story into print, I was not at all sure I could be of any help. At the time of Cathy's call, I had four political thrillers under my belt and had just finished my first contemporary novel. In short, I considered myself a novelist. I had ventured into nonfiction to write political humor, but that was a long way from assisting someone with his biography.

Cathy knew my soft spot—music. In all my books, music plays a central role with the main characters. "Just listen to him sing," she implored. "You're going to love his music."

So, I watched the YouTube video of Landau's audition for *America's Got Talent* and—like the fans of the show—was instantly hooked. I stayed up late that night watching videos of every song he sang on *America's Got Talent*. I downloaded his album, *That's Life,* and listened as I started reading interviews and articles on Landau's remarkable rags-to-riches life story.

It didn't take me too long to realize that Landau's story was better than a novel—because it was real. The highs in Landau's life were skyward and his lows were deeper than the depths of the greatest ocean. In fact, if you tried to tell Landau's story as a novel, it probably wouldn't sell, because no one would believe it.

I changed my tune. I had to meet Landau. I wanted to hear him live. Most importantly, I was dying to be the one to help Landau tell his story. Instead of thinking about excuses of why I was probably not the right person to help with this book, I began campaigning for the job and was excited when I got it.

I jumped in a car and drove to rural West Virginia to attend a benefit concert where Landau was performing. Before I started the process of gathering the stories of his life, I simply wanted to see him in action. While I'm not quite sure what I was expecting, Landau Eugene Murphy, Jr. exceeded my wildest expectations.

Landau and I arrived at the venue about the same time and we started talking in the parking lot. Once you start talking to Landau, you feel like you've known him your whole life. He has an engaging personality that immediately draws you to him and an infectious sense of humor that makes you want to stay. His smile is real. By the time we reached the stage door, we were laughing and cutting up like old friends.

Once inside the hall, Landau's band (a collection of very talented musicians) was already tuned up and ready to play. There was a choir of high school singers sitting in the first three rows waiting to rehearse *Silent Night* with Landau for the evening's encore. When Landau stepped on stage for the sound check, he was all smiles. In fact, I don't think I've ever seen anyone have as much fun on a sound check as Landau. He was laughing, cutting up with the other musicians, and interacting with the high school kids. A high five to one of them made him the envy of all his classmates.

What was so great was you could tell it wasn't an act. Landau was having a blast.

During one of the breaks, I struck up a conversation with the band's piano player Sean Parsons. I asked Sean if Landau always had this much fun at sound check. He laughed and said Landau was the consummate performer. Then he paid his front man what may be the best compliment a musician can give to a performer. He said, "If Landau thinks there is one person listening to him singing, he's putting on a show."

Landau's guitar player, Dale Roberts, offered similar praise. "Landau takes us all to another level," he told me as he tuned up his ax.

And if I thought Landau's sound check was fun, the show itself was a new level of excitement. He sang and told stories about being on *America's Got Talent* to a sell out crowd of over 3,000 folks. At one point in the show, he slipped around to the back of the room with a cordless microphone and began walking through the crowd while singing. When the show was over, he sat at a table for two more hours signing autographs and posing for pictures for anyone who wanted one.

It was fun to watch Landau find a connection with his audience because it transcended the music itself. It's easy to understand why. He's West Virginia's Everyman—a Phoenix who has risen up from the ashes of poverty on a dream as big as the mountains themselves.

Landau Eugene Murphy, Jr. is a performer who lives up to his hype. There's nothing phony about the guy. He smiles and you believe. Landau dreamed big and it paid off. But he knows it was the fans who made his dream come true. He's as sincere in his appreciation of his fans as it appears on stage and television.

This is going to be fun.

Rick Robinson
Ripley, West Virginia
December 14, 2012

"We gonna rock."

—Patti LaBelle, June 3, 2013

Chapter One

The funny thing is, I didn't enter *America's Got Talent* expecting that I would win.

Most folks who know me don't believe me when I make that claim. When it comes to my singing abilities, I'm a pretty confident guy. In one way or another, I've been performing—singing and dancing—my entire life. And when I have an audience in front of me, I know I can own the moment. But, when you understand the set of circumstances that led to me sitting down in front of a computer and filling out the on-line application for *America's Got Talent*, maybe you'll understand why I had no expectation of winning.

In many respects, I've always been an entertainer. My earliest memories as a kid are of dancing for my parents and friends and winning talent shows in elementary school. Later in life, I sang in bands and performed at charity benefits. So, to some degree, I had been working up to my "big break" for a lifetime. Still, when I applied to be on *America's Got Talent*, I didn't think I could win.

You see, as confident as I was about my talent as an entertainer, I convinced myself I didn't have "the look" to be the big winner. In my mind, I was a skinny African-American pushing forty, with dark skin, buckteeth and dreads. Maybe it was the taunts of being called "Buckwheat" as a kid, but I was very self-conscious about my appearance. I figured the show was looking for someone with a more mainstream appeal—a kid maybe. Anyway, I didn't think I had the looks to win.

I truly believe God has a plan for each of us, and if we listen to our heart, He will lead us down the right path. That's why I have trouble singing gospel songs—I get too choked up when I sing them. If anything, my story is about listening for God's direction. Looking back, there are so many times He spoke to me. There are times when I listened and times when I didn't. Thankfully, he never gave up on me.

Don't get me wrong, I did believe that somehow *America's Got Talent* was going to change my fortune in life. But when I applied for the show, my goal was just hoping to make it to the first audition on television. I was certain if I could get on television, someone would hear my voice and want to hire me to sing. Little did I know the dream of one television appearance would forever change my life.

At the time, my wife Jennifer and I were living in a little house in Logan, West Virginia in a little community of Whitman, near a creek named Old Copper Mine Fork. Jennifer grew up in that house and her mom gave it to her years earlier. It was near a small collection of houses where I spent my childhood, walking distance from the church where Jennifer and I were married. This little spot is my favorite place in the world, filled with so many happy memories I'd need to write two or three books to tell all my stories about growing up there.

Unfortunately, I have to start the book with a bad story, because it's what led me to *America's Got Talent*.

The house was a big deal to Jennifer and me. I had done some work on the place to fix it up—put in new light fixtures, tiled the bathroom—stuff like that to make the place feel more like home to us.

I was working various day jobs—like washing cars—and focusing on developing a music career in the evenings. In order to work on my music, I bought an eight track mixer/recorder and built a makeshift recording studio. It sounds funny now, but I lined the walls of one of our closets with egg cartons and hung a Radio Shack microphone from the ceiling. I had to close the door to the closet to record and it got really, really hot in my "studio." Still, I'd spend hours in there dubbing tracks and working on melodies.

Then Jennifer's stepfather, Wilbur "Jelly" Monroe, passed away. And one day soon after he died, Jennifer's mom, Miss Idella, called us and said she didn't want to be alone. Of course, we didn't hesitate. We threw some clothes in the car (along with my mixer and microphone) and went to Miss Idella's house. We stayed over night with her so she wouldn't get lonely. One night turned into two and, before we knew it, we'd been there a week or more.

Eventually Jennifer and I had to go back home to get some clothes. So we headed back to our house. When we pulled up in front of our place, I couldn't believe my eyes. It didn't take us long to figure out that someone had broken in and robbed us. The door was kicked in and there was water running down the front steps. We walked into the house and the place was a disaster area. All the appliances were gone. When they took the washing machine, they hadn't even bothered to unhook it. Water was shooting out of the busted pipes onto the floor. I had no idea how long the water had been running, but it didn't matter much anyway. Everything in sight was drenched.

As we walked around the house it got worse. The people had stolen almost everything. Our clothes were gone. Our pictures were gone. What furniture they hadn't taken was smashed on the floor. They even took the copper pipes out of the walls. As an added insult, they kicked holes in the walls and tore up the tile I had put down in the bathroom. The place was a wreck and we lost everything. We went back to Jennifer's mom's house dejected and worried about how we could ever recover from such a blow.

Little did we know things would get worse before they got better.

At the time, Jennifer was the manager of a local restaurant. We were very close friends with the owner. When he was trying to figure out a way to get more people to have dinner there on the weekends, Jennifer told him I was a singer. After he heard me sing, I was hired to perform three nights a week. It was the perfect job for both Jennifer and me. She worked the front while I packed them in singing to the tracks I mixed in my closet studio.

Just before our house was broken into, the owner passed away and the new management decided I was making too much money, a whopping $250 a night. I was setting up my equipment when the new owners told Jennifer that they were reducing my pay to $50—not a night, but for all three nights combined. I loved singing at that place and enjoyed working with my wife, but I wasn't about to perform for tips. I packed my equipment and walked out.

My prospects for other singing gigs in and around Logan were not real bright. The band I was once part of called, Top Shelf, broke up long before and no other place was looking for a solo act.

One day I was all alone at Miss Idella's house when I went into a rage. There I was, unemployed with no hope of finding the kind of job I wanted. And we lost everything to people who broke into our house. About the only things we owned were the clothes on our backs and my mixes in my recorder. I began yelling at God, telling Him I had reformed my life and done all that He had asked me to do. I was angry that in return, He left me standing there without a dime or a prospect.

People always talk about God speaking to them. Well, on that day, He spoke to me in a voice as clear as can be. I was crying and yelling like a madman when a voice said, "I've given you all the talent in the world. All you need is a bigger stage."

I froze in my tracks and looked up. I wiped the tears from my face and thought about the words. All my life everyone told me my voice was a gift from God. Now God was telling me the same thing. Suddenly all the anger and rage seemed to leave my body and I felt an inner peace. I wasn't sure what was going to happen, but I knew instantly everything was going to be all right.

All you need is a bigger stage.

The words swirled around in my head as I tried to figure out what He was trying to tell me. I had performed at charity events around Logan for years making a name for myself. Maybe God was telling me to move on to some place bigger. I lived in Detroit for a part of my youth and didn't want to move to a big city. I loved Logan and I could never even think about moving from here.

What happened next makes most folks laugh, but I swear it happened.

As I walked around the room trying to figure out the whole idea of a bigger stage, a commercial came on the television for *America's Got Talent*. One of my childhood heroes, Howie Mandel, was talking about his television show and asked the question, "Could you be the next grand prize winner of *America's Got Talent?* Do you have what it takes to be our million dollar winner and headline your own show in Las Vegas?"

I froze and a cold chill came over me as I uttered "YES."

I understand why people find this story funny. Of course, it doesn't help when I tell them God spoke to me and He sounded just like Howie Mandel.

I waited for the commercial to end and I quickly memorized the website address. Then I ran upstairs, turned on my mother-in-law's computer and read everything I could on the website about the show. I filled out the online application. When I clicked the "submit" button, I was relieved. I knew my life was somehow going to be changed forever.

That night, Jennifer got home early from working at the restaurant. She was crying and real upset. The restaurant fired her. The same new management that let me go as their singer fired my wife.

Surprisingly, I was not mad or angry. In fact, I laughed it off. I thought this was all part of God's plan for me.

After Jennifer told me the whole story about being let go, I sat her down and told her what happened to me that day. I tried to comfort her about the fact we were now both unemployed and tried to assure her not to worry. I told her everything was going to be okay.

"I am about to find a bigger stage," I declared. "I'm going to audition for *America's Got Talent*. Someone will see me on television and hire me as a singer."

Now most any wife would think her husband was nuts for coming up with such a crazy plan for their future. But somehow, I convinced Jennifer this was our destiny. And even though I didn't think I could win, I knew I just did something to better our lives.

That day started the strangest journey I've ever taken.

"I really don't think most people realize just how talented Landau is."

— Glenn Leonard, former lead vocalist for the Temptations

Chapter Two

Every day I checked my email account two or three times looking for a reply from the talent scouts at *America's Got Talent*.
Apparently, no one told them my destiny was hanging in the bal-
ance. Each minute between each check seemed like a lifetime.

I spent a lot of time mixing tapes and working on various rendi-
tions of songs. One of the things I started doing was helping kids in
the neighborhood write and record their own rap mixes. My sister
always had us perform for our parents when we were kids, so I
really got into having kids hang around and create music. I'd have
them sit down at Miss Idella's kitchen table and write out their raps
on paper. The first one done would get to record first. So they
would rush through writing them and then I'd turn on a beat. When
they were done, I'd give them a CD of their song to take home and
play for their parents and friends.

Jennifer and I didn't have two dimes to rub together and some
of my family thought I shouldn't be giving kids free CDs. But I've
always believed in giving back to my community. Even though we
were broke, I felt like helping kids make music was a way I could
give back a little bit.

It took a month or two, but I finally got an email from someone
at *America's Got Talent* setting the date for my pre-audition. The
pre-audition is the chance for talent scouts with the show to decide
which performers get a call back for the televised audition. The
pre-audition was a couple of months down the road, which turned
out to be a good thing for us. The pre-audition location was the Big
Apple—New York City.

New York was iffy for us. We flat out didn't have the money to
get there, let alone money for a room and food while we were

there. A lot of family and friends helped us out, but two of my friends in particular really stepped up for us—Mike Ferrell and Rick Lowe.

Up to this point in my life, I'd worked many different jobs—from cutting hair in my basement to flagging for a construction crew. But one of the jobs I'd done over the years was detailing cars for dealerships. I've waxed so many hoods and scrubbed so many tires that I used to dream at night about being up to my neck in bubbles.

So, I called Mike Ferrell, who owns the Toyota dealership up in Chapmanville, West Virginia. I told Mike about my crazy plan to go to New York for a pre-audition and explained that I needed to save up money to get there. I worked for Mike a few years earlier, and he was one of those folks who believed in me and my talent. I think back now and laugh about my pitch to him, "Please hire me so I can become famous and quit." For some reason Mike agreed to rehire me as a car detailer and I started shoving my hands into cold spray and water again.

Jennifer and I started to scrape together every penny we could in an attempt to come up with what we needed to get to New York. My mom, Mona Lisa (just like the Nat "King" Cole song "Mona Lisa Lost Her Smile"), gave us some money and I saved everything I could from my job at Mike Ferrell Toyota. Still, we were not going to have enough to get to The Big Apple.

Remember that before my job as a restaurant singer, I was in a five-piece blues and soul band called Top Shelf? My little brother introduced me to this piano player and band leader named Rick Lowe who owned a local grocery store and was looking for a front man for his band. We hit it off and named the band. For a time, I traveled around West Virginia's back roads singing in smoky bars and clubs. Like all bands, we had our troubles. I wanted to add some crooner tunes to the set list and they wanted to stay true to the R&B format we had been performing. In the end, they wanted to continue to sing "My Girl" and I wanted to start singing "Fly Me to the Moon." When we broke up, I remained friends with Rick and his wife Penny.

Thankfully for Rick, the band was not his only source of income. He was successful in real estate along with his grocery business. When it became clear we were not going to have enough money to make it to New York, I called Rick. He gladly gave us the rest of the money we needed and we made plans to head to the Big Apple for the pre-audition of *America's Got Talent*.

On November 16, 2010, I made sure we got up early so we could be one of the first ones in line for the pre-audition. At 5:00 a.m. we headed out for the walk from the Holiday Inn Express to the Javits Convention Center. My plan didn't work out so well. When we got to the Javits, the line already stretched out for several blocks. Looking back at it, I bet some of those folks got in line the day before.

So Jennifer and I got in line and watched as people continued to get in line behind us. My showing up early turned out to be late, but at least we weren't at the back of the line. It was a couple of hours later when I realized the people around us were all wearing yellow wristbands. I checked it out and, sure enough, all the contestants had to check-in and get wristbands with numbers on them. I figured out where to register, got the wristband, and slinked to the back of a never ending line.

I tried to remain cool as the line slowly made its way to the Javits Convention Center, but I couldn't quit thinking about the stupid mistake I made with the wristbands. This was going to be a long day. Some people started performing in line. Others just gave up and got out of line. But even though our feet were hurting, I refused to give up. I knew this was my chance to better my life and I wasn't going to let it slip away.

In order to keep my self together, I started thinking about all the folks back in West Virginia who believed in me—my mom, my kids—everybody in Logan. I also started thinking about all the times people told me my voice was a gift from God. One particular time kept running through my head.

Like all people, my life has not been perfect and I've made mistakes that I'd like to take back. One day, when I was in my twenties, I got into a fight on a basketball court in Detroit, Michigan. Street games can often get physical, but this one ended in a scuffle.

Unbeknownst to me at the time, the person I fought with filed assault charges against me.

I say "unbeknownst to me," because I never knew about the charges until I ended up getting pulled over for speeding one day and the police officer informed me there was an outstanding warrant for my arrest. Well, off to jail I went.

I was sitting in the holding cell and, as I often do when I'm nervous, I started to sing. I remember it so clearly; I was singing "My Girl" by The Temptations. This big dude walked up to me in the cell and asked me what I was doing there. He was huge, with big arms and a bald head—very, very scary looking.

I told him I had been arrested for fighting on the basketball court. When he asked me to sing, I did "My Girl" from start to finish.

The big dude then looked at one guy in the cell and asked him how old he was. "Fifty," the guy responded. He kept asking everyone around us their age. I was the youngest guy in the room.

"Boy," he said to me in a very stern voice, "look at the people in this jail cell with you. This is your life if you don't straighten up your act."

I wasn't sure where he was going, but I sure wasn't going to interrupt.

"It's too late for all of us," he said. "You got a voice that is a gift from God and it will be wasted if you end up in here. Understand?"

"Yes, sir," was all I could mutter.

He then told me to ask people on the street about him. He said he had a pretty tough reputation and folks had a right to be scared of him. "A voice like that and you're in here," he snarled. "If I ever catch you back in jail, I'll kill ya myself."

I never asked around the street about his reputation. I didn't have to. I believed him. And I never went back to jail.

About 6:00 p.m. we made it inside the Javits Convention Center. Finally, I thought I was getting close to singing—no such luck. Once inside the building there were more lines and even more waiting and no food. We were starting to get hungry. Around 9:00 p.m., about 16 hours after we left our hotel room, they called my number. The staff for the show took a bunch of us into a separate room and divided us up by our talents. Musicians went in one direction. Performers went in another. I went into a room with about thirty other singers.

When I sat down in the room, I sat where I thought I'd be first up to perform. The talent scout had other ideas and started at the other end. Instead of first, I was going to be last. I had waited all day long—another couple of minutes weren't going to mess things up. And being last ended up being a good thing for me, because I got to watch how the talent scouts reacted to all the other singers. Many of the singers had great voices, but were showing no confidence in their performance. I decided when it was my turn, I was going to put on a show.

I had read the rules for the pre-audition indicating that performers were allowed to bring recorded music. When I got in front of the talent scouts, I pulled out my CD mix for a short version of "I've Got You Under My Skin." Of course, the way my luck had gone that day, I should have figured they would not be able to find a working CD player. Rather than asking the talent scouts to go find a player, I decided to go acapella.

So, I looked down at the floor and tried to block everything out. I started tapping my foot and snapping my fingers to set the beat. I've got long fingers and can snap really loud. Then, swinging my dreadlocks as I started, I launched into "I've Got You Under My Skin."

While I was singing, I moved around like I was singing to the biggest audience I'd ever played before. I was snapping my fingers, swinging my dreads and singing with as much soul as I could muster. It worked. The other singers in the room were standing up and dancing along with me. One of the talent scouts was tapping out a beat with her pencil. Another one was smiling and nodding to the beat. When I finished, all the other performers in the room applauded and started slapping me on the back.

One of the talent scouts, a guy named Mike Farrell (that's right; the exact same name as my old boss back home) paused for a minute, stood up and told us that the audition was over. He gave us all the old, "don't call us, we'll call you," speech. I thought it was more than a coincidence he had the same name as the man I washed cars for back in West Virginia who helped pay my way to the audition. I had to do something else to get his attention. I knew in my gut if I walked out of that room, none of us would ever get a call back.

As we all started to walk out the door, I began loudly singing one of the tunes from our Top Shelf set—"Country Side of Life" by southern rockers Wet Willie.

You can have your buildings and your heavy arithmetic
I don't need no crowded streets or city slicker tricks
I just need to be someplace where I can move around
Look down at my toes and I can still see the ground

Gimme that country side of life
Which way I can stretch out right
Gimme the countryside ooh lord
That country side of life
Which way I don't get uptight
Gimme the countryside…of life!

Everyone walking out of the room was dancing, giving me high-fives as they left the room.

I looked back around and made eye contact with Mike Farrell. He was smiling. "Mr. Murphy, come back in here," he said. He said he was one of the producers for *America's Got Talent*.

"Yes, sir," I replied, trying hard to suppress my own grin.

"What other kind of genres do you sing?"

"All of them," I replied.

Producer Farrell paused for a minute. "Stick with the Rat Pack stuff," he said, "and you can win the whole thing." He instructed me to go sit in the hallway. My group of performers were his next to last for the evening and he wanted me to stick around for a screen test. I was elated. It was happening.

I sat down on a chair in the hallway and watched the last group walk into the room. When I noticed one of people in the last group was a white guy dressed like Sammy Davis, Jr., I started to laugh.

Jennifer was still sitting in a holding room outside the audition room and she saw the people I went in with come out. She was getting excited and tiptoed around the corner to find me sitting alone in the hall. "They want me to go to the big producer's room," I said excitedly. She gave me a big hug and tiptoed back out.

After he finished with the last group, Mike from *America's Got Talent* took me down to the production room and kept telling me to stick with the Rat Pack stuff. They pulled a couple of other people out for screen tests and I watched as they performed. When it became my turn, we found a player for my performance CD.

I don't remember much about the screen test except a stage hand giving me a "thumbs-up" after I finished as he looked at Mike and asked, "Who is this dude?"

Producer Farrell had me sign a confidentiality agreement to appear on the televised audition show. Then, he gave me the best piece of advice I ever got, "Go home and don't leave your bedroom."

"Sometimes I hear him and look around to see if Frank Sinatra is here. But, hey man, he's dead. This is Landau."

—Steve Tyrell, Grammy award winning producer and artist while recording Landau's debut CD "That's Life"

Chapter Three

When I was a kid someone nicknamed me "Doonie." I'm not really sure where it came from or who gave it to me. I have always supposed it was some strange variation of the last syllable of my name, Landau. It's not exactly the same, but Doonie probably sounded better than Downey. No matter how it came about, all my life I've been known to my family and close friends as Doonie.

When I went to the pre-audition in New York City, I was going to use my nickname as part of my hook by calling myself "Doonie Tunes," a play on the cartoons of my youth. As Doonie Tunes I was going to sing a wide variety of music, not just Sinatra. I expected I would lead off as a crooner. If I was lucky enough to make it to Las Vegas and beyond, I'd sing some Motown and maybe even one of the southern rock songs I used to perform with Top Shelf.

I came up with that plan before I met *America's Got Talent* producer Mike Farrell. When I was doing the screen test, he kept telling me over and over again that if I stuck with the Rat Pack theme, I had a chance to win the whole thing. I dropped the Doonie Tunes idea and decided to stick with the crooner theme.

Producer Farrell gave me another great piece of advice when he told me to go back to Logan and stay in my room. For the next couple of months, Jennifer and I kept by ourselves as much as possible. It worked most of the time.

When I got back to West Virginia, I was allowed to tell folks I was going to be on the audition for *America's Got Talent*, but not much else. Everybody was peppering me with questions, but I kept my mouth shut. I certainly didn't tell anyone that one of the producers thought I had a shot at winning by sticking with Sinatra. At the time, I'm not sure I believed him, but I still decided to follow the suggestion. And that caused me a lot of grief over the next couple of months.

Everybody seemed to have an opinion on what kind of music I should sing at the audition. So many people thought I was blowing my big chance by singing Sinatra. Most of them thought I should be singing rhythm and blues instead of crooner songs. Before we went to New York for the audition, I had a cousin who got really upset with me because I wouldn't move on what I was going to sing. He called me a fool and said the show was never going to accept a black man singing Sinatra. I just kept quiet and looked forward to getting to New York for the audition.

The televised audition for *America's Got Talent* was April 1, 2011—April Fools Day. The date seemed pretty appropriate to me. Here I was, a black kid with dreadlocks from West Virginia, in Frank Sinatra's old stomping grounds, "New York, New York," getting ready to try to sing songs like 'Ol' Blue Eyes' himself.

This time the show put us up at a nice hotel near Central Park. But I was more nervous for this audition than I was back in the fall. At the pre-audition, I was performing in front of talent scouts. This time I was going to be performing in front of a live audience and was being recorded for television. And I was still concerned about not having "the look" for the show.

One of the things I was worried about was embarrassing West Virginia. There are a lot of people who go onto reality television shows and make fools of themselves. I did not want that to happen to me. I was sincerely worried some people might take me the wrong way. Let's face it, when you see me for the first time, crooner is not exactly the word that comes to mind.

The night of the audition, I was the next-to-last act to perform. They made it look on the television replay like I was the last act and in a way I was. Because of the fumes that would be generated, they actually had the motorcycle act go last. I was the last act that didn't involve putting a whole bunch of fumes into the theater.

I was standing backstage trying to calm down. My hands sweat real bad right before I perform and I was trying to get myself together before I walked onto the stage. I forgot I had to stop and talk to show host, Nick Cannon ("Mr. Mariah Carey"), on the way out to the stage. I actually walked past him when he grabbed me to do my pre-performance interview. I was so nervous from the interview I forgot to toss my gum into the garbage can before I walked onto the stage. Of course, that led to one of the funnier moments of the audition when Piers Morgan told me to spit out my gum and I had no place to put it except my pants pocket.

Seeing Howie Mandel calmed me down. I had been a big Howie Mandel fan ever since I watched his cartoon *Bobby's World* when I was a kid. I loved that show. When I walked on stage and saw him sitting there, I just busted out laughing. I'm not sure why but I blurted out my Bobby impersonation.

I really think that Howie and the other two judges—Piers Morgan and Sharon Osbourne—had no idea what to expect from me. I was wearing jeans, a corduroy jacket and a pair of PF Flyer tennis shoes. They certainly didn't expect to hear Sinatra that night.

There were no speakers on the stage for the performers to hear their voice and once I hit the first note and started singing, the crowd was so loud I couldn't hear myself. I could actually feel the vibrations from the roar of the crowd in my chest. I wasn't the only one who couldn't hear. My wife Jennifer said the crowd was so loud she couldn't hear either. Everything after the first note was purely by instinct. I couldn't hear a thing. The crowd was screaming. It was great. It was exhilarating.

In the television version of the audition, it looked like I was only on stage for a couple of minutes after I performed. But, in reality, they kept me on stage for a long time. It seemed like hours, but I think it was only about forty-five minutes. Piers, Sharon and Howie just kept talking to me and asking questions. All the while, the crowd kept cheering, shouting my name and chanting "vote, vote, vote." The producer kept telling the crowd to be quiet, but they just went on shouting and making noise. At one point, they threatened to start kicking people out of the theater if they didn't shut up.

It was all so overwhelming to me at the time. I went to New York City not expecting to win and only hoping I would get on television and have someone see me sing. Yet here was the audience cheering for me. I was worried about not having the look the show was searching for in a winner, but here they were—cheering for me.

When Howie Mandel looked at me and said my life would never be the same, it hit me. I didn't have to look like somebody else. I didn't have to conform to what people wanted me to be. I could be myself and follow my dream.

And, of course, that's when I started crying.

While the last act was on stage, I went backstage and shot some B-roll for the television show. Twenty-four hours before that, I had no idea what "B" roll even was! I called my mom back in West Virginia and she was thrilled.

All this time my wife, Jennifer, had been sitting up in the balcony of the theater. She was up there with her niece, Christina Brasher, and my friends Francine and Prince Moore from the New York area, a couple I used to sing with back in 2005. When I finished with everything they wanted me to do backstage, I slipped up to the balcony and sat behind them while the motorcycle act ended their performance. When they turned around to leave, there I was. Jennifer screamed and we hugged, and we all had a good time celebrating that I was going to be headed to Las Vegas for the second show.

I didn't expect what happened next because I had stayed with Jennifer up in the balcony for the last act. I walked downstairs into the lobby of the theater where all of the people who had just seen the show were in line getting their cell phones back from security. The show doesn't let people take their cell phones in to the audition. Suddenly, everybody started grabbing their phones from security and rushing over to Jennifer and me to snap pictures. People started grabbing at us.

One of the security people for the theater came over and asked if we had a car waiting for us. When I said we didn't, he got another security guard and the two of them told us they needed to get us out of here or there was going to be a riot. People were pushing and shoving try to get pictures, and these two security guards shoved us out the front door and into a cab.

Only an hour earlier, Howie Mandel told me that my life was never going to be the same again. And here I was being mobbed by people outside the theater.

Jennifer and I went back to Logan and didn't tell anybody anything. Everybody in town knew I was going to be on television, but I kept my mouth shut. Whenever anyone asked what happened in New York, I just smiled and thought to myself, *I know something you don't know.*

People started setting up parties to watch the audition and a lot of people started inviting me to their particular party. I turned them all down.

Then, they started running commercials for the show and they showed a clip of me crying. A lot of folks assumed from the clip that I was crying because I hadn't made it to the next round. I guess they never thought I was crying tears of pure joy rather than tears of agony.

Anyway, my audition for *America's Got Talent* aired on May 31st—Jennifer's birthday. And, as they say, the rest is history. My phone started ringing as soon as the show was over and hasn't stopped ringing yet. I had time for a quick "victory lap" in Logan with my friends and family and I was soon on a plane to Las Vegas, Nevada for round two.

Howie was right. My life has never been the same.

"Landau was a positive story for West Virginia at a time when West Virginia was in desperate need of a positive story."

—Dave Allen, Program Director and
Morning Show Host WVOW,
Logan, WV

Chapter Four

My life has changed dramatically since I appeared on the audition for *America's Got Talent*. In lots of ways, I'm still just the guy from Logan, West Virginia who stood in line for sixteen hours at the Javits Center to audition for the show. What has changed is my world is now a little larger than Logan. To make it easier for you to understand what I mean, I should probably tell you a little bit about my life.

I was born on August 11, 1974 in Logan, West Virginia – the fourth of five children to Landau and Mona Lisa Murphy. Many people hear my life story and call it a tough road. And I guess it has been to some degree. Dad was a coal miner and we struggled every month to get by. But, a life grounded in music is a happy life. From as far back as I can remember, music was a part of my life. I can't remember a time without a beat. Whether it was my parents playing records with their friends or my sister leading dance lines, there was always rhythm around our house. I was born singing and dancing.

Apparently, I also have it in my blood. My grandfather, Reverend Cecil Murphy, was part of a gospel singing group, The Pioneer Five. I never saw him perform but I've seen pictures of them all done up in top hats, tails, and canes.

My parents had a big influence on my life. Both of them loved music. Dad had this kind of "man cave" in the basement of our house in Logan and it became the center of my young musical universe. The room had a real 70s "Black Panther" feel to it. The walls were painted dark red and there were yellow peace symbols and paintings of African men and women all over the walls. Today they'd call it nostalgia or pop art. We called it home.

The room was filled with musical instruments and equipment. Dad played bass guitar, but there was a set of drums and keyboards and all kinds of amps around the room. Dad's friends would come over to the house and they'd play music until all hours in the basement. I used to love it when they'd all start jamming. The rhythm and beat were the pulse that fueled my youth. If I wasn't down in the basement with the musicians, I was in my room singing along.

Dad and his friends played a lot of funk and Motown. Sometimes, they would play some Hendrix, so I got exposed to everything from rhythm and blues to rock. Even though they wouldn't let me touch the equipment, I liked to sit around in the basement and listen to them play. Well, sit isn't the right word. Those jam sessions are where I started to learn how to dance. The men would play and I'd dance. Occasionally, probably just to make me stop dancing, somebody would hand me a shaker or a tambourine and I'd slap out the beat.

The basement wasn't the only place where I found a beat. When dad and his buddies weren't playing live downstairs, my mom was upstairs in the living room spinning records. There was a steady stream of Marvin Gaye, Earth Wind and Fire and, of course, Stevie Wonder – who was like a god around our house. The tunes of my parents' favorite artists became the foundation of what I like in music too.

If artists from my parents' era were my foundation, my biggest influence as a kid came from the King of Pop – Michael Jackson. My parents had some old Jackson 5 albums we'd listen to from time to time. Then one day I saw Michael Jackson on *Night Tracks* on TBS, and I was mesmerized by the way he danced. Michael Jackson suddenly became everything to me. I'd hang out in front of the television just hoping to see a Michael Jackson video. I taught myself to moonwalk and learned all of MJ's dance moves. Everywhere I went, I was bustin' moves – moonwalking, spinning, and balancing up on my toes. I could do every move to every one of his videos on MTV – "Billie Jean," "Beat It," the monster moves from "Thriller." I had them all.

And, that's when I first started performing.

Mom and Dad loved to go out to the clubs around Logan, which at the time were still basically segregated. Their favorite was a juke joint called the Wonder Club. Almost every Saturday night they'd go out to listen to live bands and dance with their friends. When the clubs would shut down, on most nights the party would move back to our house. My brother and I would mess around the house until we knew it was about time for our parents to get home. Then we'd go back to our bedroom and act like we were asleep. What we were really doing was waiting for the car to pull up in front of the house and for the party to start.

It was never quiet when Mom and Dad got back from the clubs. They'd start out trying to keep their voices down, but then someone would tell a joke and everybody would laugh. Pretty soon all the grown ups would be talking loud and the party was on. My Mom would put on an Ohio Players album and my Dad would start singing the band's "Skin Tight" at the top of his lungs. It didn't take long until everybody was singing and dancing in the living room. My brother and I still made believe we were sleeping, but we were actually in our rooms singing, too.

At some point my Dad would call out my name and tell me to come out to the living room. He probably knew I was awake anyway. Still, I would come walking down the hall acting like I had been asleep, rubbing my eyes and yawning a fake yawn. People would start telling me to dance for them. So they'd put on a Michael Jackson album and I'd start to dance. It seems so funny now, because there I was in my Spiderman underwear and ragged T-shirt dancing the whole song routine while my parents and their rowdy friends cheered me on.

They always liked to play "Billie Jean" and I loved to dance to it. When the song would finish, I would moonwalk backwards out the door to the room, stop and salute. The adults would roar their approval. A couple of them would each give me a dollar for my efforts. Looking back at it, I guess dancing for my Mom and Dad's friends was my first paying gig. I would have done it for nothing. I loved the music and I loved putting on a show.

Looking back on it now, I was probably always destined to be an entertainer. I started performing in front of people at an early age and, in a picture of things to come, I even started entering talent shows. One year I won the Halloween dance contest at my elementary school. I still remember it – I dressed up just like Michael Jackson and performed his routine to "Billie Jean." First Place was a plastic spoon from Dairy Queen. Our family friend Jackie Bass took me into town where I got to trade in the spoon for a free ice-cream sundae.

After one of those shows I'd won, the lady we called the "Candy Lady" snapped a picture of me flashing a "Number One" sign with my right index finger. Years later, my mom found that photo and showed it to me after I flashed the same sign for winning *America's Got Talent*. I'm not sure if it was a sign of things to come, but looking at the two pictures side by side is makes me wonder if God didn't have this planned for me all along.

The first several years of school I went to Holden Elementary where I was one of the few black kids in my class. I didn't have a problem with it and neither did anyone else, at least as far as I knew. We were all poor kids from a coal mining area of West Virginia. When our daddies came out of the mine covered in coal dust, they were all black. It was just the way it was for me. In the day, I'd go to school with my friends and try to pay attention. But, the outdoors was always really calling me. Then in the afternoon we'd all play down in the creek by our house. We did stuff like other kids – watched cartoons and things – but since we were living in West Virginia, we also had the mountains as our playground. I used to run through the woods in the mountains like I owned them.

When we would play, my sister, Pam, was always the leader. If we played school, she would be the teacher. If we played hide-and-go-seek, Pam got to decide who had to be "it" first. I guess she was my first producer/director.

Pam really, really liked to teach us dance routines. She would work up a routine to some dance song like "Second Time Around" or "Disco Inferno" and we'd all have to dance the routine. My brothers and sisters would all do what Pam told them. Of course, I would be the one who would act up. I never wanted to be just another dancer in the line. I wanted the dance to be all about me.

While I was still in elementary school, Mom and Dad split up. After that, we moved to Columbus, Ohio for about a year. Nothing against all the *America's Got Talent* fans who voted for me in Columbus, but at the time I really hated it there. All my friends were back in Logan and there were no mountains. All I could think about while living there was moving back home.

I probably have some bad feelings about living in Columbus because of a fight I got into there during one of my first days at school. I was on the playground just humming a tune and watching some other kids play tether ball when Reggie, a kid who lived down the street from us, walked up and just started punching me in the stomach. It wasn't really a fight. A fight is where two people throw punches. For some reason, I didn't hit Reggie back. I was so stunned at the time. He had his chin all stuck out and hit me six or seven times in the stomach. Reggie was supposed to be my friend and he was hitting me for no apparent reason. I started crying and walked away.

Later in the school year, Reggie had a bad fall at school while trying to slide down a handrail. He fell a couple of floors, landed on his head and got messed up real bad. In retrospect, maybe my time in Columbus wasn't so bad after all. I guess I got my first lesson in Karma there.

On the upside, while I was going to school in Columbus, I learned how to wink at a girl. I was going to Hubbard Elementary School and there was this cute girl in one of my classes. I wanted her to be my girlfriend so I winked at her. Okay, that sounds pretty funny today, but it was the best plan I could come up with at the time. That wink was the longest, most nervous wink in the history of mankind.

I was real excited when we moved back to Logan. It was about this time when I started getting a real interest in basketball. It started when my brothers would fill up a sock with paper and we would play around the living room on our knees like we were shooting hoops. My older brothers never gave me a break when we played. They'd push me around and make me earn my scores. That's what ended up making me such an aggressive player when I got older.

One summer we put a peach basket up on a tree behind our house. It was a grass court but we played basketball on it so much the ground started to get hard. We didn't have a real basketball. Instead we played with one of those red balls you'd use to play four-square. It was real bouncy, but then again, we were playing on grass, not concrete. I started to play basketball whenever I had the chance.

I was also still winning talent shows for dancing. I just kept doing everything like Michael Jackson. Somebody bought me an outfit like Michael's to wear to competitions. I wore a sequined glove on one hand. I even had a little Jeri curl down the front of my forehead. Years later, when the robbers broke in and took everything from our house, that picture of me with a Jeri-curl is one item I'm glad they took! The evidence is gone.

Mom and Dad's split up was real tough on me. Mom started dating a new guy. I missed Dad, but I really liked Mom's new boyfriend. He wasn't into music like my real dad, but he was very good to me.

One day, he and Mom packed us in a car to go to a family reunion in Dayton, Ohio. That car ride led to one of the biggest changes in my life.

Chapter Five

The family reunion in Dayton, Ohio was a lot of fun. There were lots of kids around. We played basketball all day long and had a huge meal. When the reunion was over, my brothers and sisters and I were exhausted. We all piled into the back seat of the car and went to sleep on what I thought would be the long drive back to Logan.

Imagine how surprised I was when I woke up in Detroit, Michigan.

Mom had family in Detroit. She decided she needed a fresh start, and she decided Detroit was the place to find it. My aunt lived there and we were going to live with her until we got on our feet. That all sounds like a good plan now, but Mom had conveniently forgot to tell me about it.

As we drove to my aunt's house, I looked around the neighborhoods. Back in Logan, I was one of the few black kids in school. Suddenly, I was in a place where everyone was black. I only spotted a handful of white kids.

And, this may sound funny, but all of the playgrounds were concrete. In my old neighborhood, the playground had trees, creeks and mountains and our basketball court was grass. In this new place, the basketball courts were surrounded by rusty chain-linked fences. I had gone from one extreme to another – rural beauty to urban decay, literally overnight.

To make matters worse, in Logan I had been the King of Dance. I entered all the talent shows and nobody could beat me. All the kids at school asked me to dance for them. Well, my Auntie Rosemary in Detroit had been telling all the kids in the neighborhood about me moving in with her and telling them I was a real good dancer. That didn't sit real well with the kids. As soon as we pulled up to the curb, there was a group of kids waiting to challenge me.

I got out of the car, and this one big kid was standing there with knee and elbow pads. He looked funny because he had an extra knee pad strapped to the top of his head. He had a piece of linoleum under his arm — definitely a weird looking dude. "Yo, we heard you can dance," he said.

"You go get 'em, baby," Auntie Rosemary yelled.

I wasn't quite sure what being challenged meant, but apparently it was on. I started dancing anyway. I did my whole "Billie Jean" routine, singing as I danced. Like always, I finished the routine by moon walking backwards and saluting. The other kids were completely and utterly unimpressed.

The kid with the knee pad on his head tossed his linoleum on the ground and started break dancing. He was bustin' moves I had never even seen before. He was spinning on his back and head. It was incredible – and heartbreaking. Somebody else was better than me at dancing.

Later that same day there was a hostage situation a couple of doors down the block. Some guy had a gun up against the head of his kid. Sirens were wailing and police were jumping out of cars with their guns pulled. Everybody in my aunt's front yard hit the deck – except me. I was looking around like I was watching the *Dukes of Hazzard*. My mom ran out of the house, grabbed me and pushed me through the front door. I watched as the police shot the guy holding the gun.

From that very first day in Detroit, all I could think about was going back to Logan. My mom quickly explained to me in no uncertain terms that was not going to happen, so I tried to settle in and make the best of my new home in the 'hood.

In about a year, we moved from my aunt's house to an even rougher neighborhood on the west side of Detroit a block from the toughest projects in the city. There were lots of gangs and drug dealers in the neighborhood. I wouldn't even want to imagine how many of the kids I grew up with on the west side were either gunned down or are now in prison. In fact, the kid who challenged me on my first day in Detroit was shot in the back of the head up on the railroad tracks. Kids were always acting up in class. Our high school was so tough they had a police station in the basement.

I did my best to stay out of trouble, but I got teased a lot because of my West Virginia accent. I learned how to fight and I also learned how to play a pretty good game of basketball.

I'd learned how to play basketball back in Logan. Just like the dancing in Detroit was at another level, so was their game of basketball. And I started playing a tough, physical game. I had to. It was the only kind of game they played there.

Originally, I played on a school team, but pretty soon I realized school ball was not for me. I was just a freshman, but I was one of the best players on the team. Even the older kids on the team knew I was a good player. But no matter how hard I practiced and played, I would get into the game only for the last minute or so when we were either winning so big or losing so big it didn't matter. To this day, I have no idea why the coach wouldn't play me more. I wanted to play, so I sucked it up.

One day at practice it came to a head between the coach and me. We were playing a scrimmage, and I went in for a layup with my right hand. The defender made a nice move on me. I knew if I continued the shot with my right hand, he would block it. Instead, I switched the ball to my left hand and took the shot. It went in. The coach was furious. He blew the whistle and gathered the whole team at center court. He lectured the whole team about showboating and – I'm not making this up – he paddled me in front of my teammates.

I was shocked and embarrassed at the same time. The coach took a paddle to my behind because he thought I was showboating. And I made the darn shot!

That was it. I quit the team that day and never went back. The coach used to come into my class all the time and try to talk to me about playing for the team again. I never would play for him again.

The coach eventually became a television preacher.

Eventually, without basketball to keep me there, I lost interest in school altogether and dropped out entirely – a bad decision so many kids in my neighborhood made.

Instead of playing for the school's team, I started playing in a church league for Rosedale Park Baptist Church. I started going to church every Sunday and youth group on Friday nights. In fact, it was at church where I met my first wife. She liked basketball just as much as me. Turns out that love of hoops isn't the only thing you need to keep a marriage together and we didn't stay married long. Before we split up though, we had three great kids.

I got more than three kids from basketball. Street ball was how I first started picking up on Sinatra music. The big television show at the time was *Married with Children* with Al and Peg Bundy and the theme song was Frank Sinatra's "Love and Marriage." I loved that show and watched it all the time. I used to sing the theme song whenever I saw kids in the neighborhood holding hands and stuff. Soon I started to listen to other Sinatra tunes.

Street ball in Detroit was a tough game. It was very physical. Flying elbows were the norm. We used to play a dozen or more games a day. When we'd play that much ball, we'd get tired by the end of the day. Tempers flared all the time and fights broke out in nearly every game. I started using Sinatra tunes to calm down tense situations on the court. If I dunked on somebody, I'd start singing: "Fly me to the moon…" Instead of fighting, guys would start to laugh. It's hard to feel dissed when someone is crooning at you. Even with the singing, I still got in a lot of fights.

It was about that time my family caught a huge break. We were renting a place at the time in a really shady west side neighborhood. There was this old lady who lived across the street from us. She didn't have any family who lived around her, and my mom used to watch out for her. She'd make her meals and take her to church and stuff. My brothers and I always went to the store for her on Sunday to buy her groceries and pick up cartons of cigarettes and chewing tobacco. She smoked like a fiend and chewed tobacco like the old men at the corner liquor store. She used to spit tobacco juice from her chew out the back door. It was pretty disgusting.

When the old woman died, her daughter came to Detroit to settle her mom's estate. She came and found my mom to thank her for all we had done for her mother. There was no way this lady was going to move into the 'hood, and no one was lining up to buy houses in our area. So, in appreciation, she gave us her mom's house. It was great – we had our own house!

Of course, the house needed some work. My brothers and I washed windows for hours to get all the smoke off the walls and windows. When we took down the curtains on the front window, they felt really heavy. It turns out that the old lady didn't trust banks and she had sewn a whole bunch of money into the hems. It was like finding buried treasure. Mom took the money and put new siding on the house.

Around that time, I had really long hair. When we moved to Detroit, I had never been to a real barber. Back in Logan, my Uncle Snoop used to cut my hair. My hair was (and still is) thin and stringy, and I just continued to let it grow. One day, my brother and I asked mom to buy us a set of clippers out of the Fingerhut catalogue, so we could cut each other's hair. My brother never really used them, but I started cutting my own hair. I used to stand in front of a mirror, and hold a hand mirror with one hand, while cutting my own hair with the other. With the clippers I started learning how to cut not only my own hair but the hair of other people. I decided I wanted to become a barber. I just needed someone to practice on.

This sounds bad, but there was this blind guy in the neighborhood named Johnny. We called him "Blind Man Johnny" and he became my first "customer." He used to come up to our house for a hair cut and give me a dollar. I could never figure out how he found our house, but he did. Johnny's brother was one of the gangstas in the neighborhood, and I was always afraid if I cut Johnny's hair bad, his brother would get somebody to shoot up our house. But I never messed up Johnny's hair and he became another musical influence in my life.

Johnny played congas and he used to play for me all the time. He taught me the differences in rhythms as he played. He was amazing and could play anything on the congas. Johnny also used to take me to church with him on Sundays. I'm not talking about regular church, but a rundown storefront called the House of Praise where people would minister to the faithful and sing for hours on Sunday.

When we played basketball later in the day, Johnny would come along with us. Every week, I'd put him into the game for a few minutes. I know – like I said, he was blind. But his hearing and instincts were so good, he could actually follow the ball and the flow of the game. If he heard someone on the other team dribbling, he would run up to them and start poking his hands at the sound of the dribble. Having a blind guy run up and start poking at the ball used to scare the crap out of new guys, and we used to laugh our butts off.

One day I told Johnny about riding my bike around the neighborhood. He started asking me all kinds of questions about what it felt like. "You mean no one ever put you on a bike before?"

"Nope," Johnny replied.

It sounds crazy now, but I took Johnny out to the street and put him on my bike. I put his hands on the handlebars, his feet on the pedals and started walking him down the street. He wanted to go faster, so I started running. Suddenly, he started pedaling real fast and pulled away from me. It must have looked funny to see me running behind a blind guy on a bicycle. He went a whole block by himself before he stopped. When I caught up with him, I was out of breath. I was going to yell at him for taking off. Then I noticed he was crying. He told me that riding a bike was something he had always wanted to do. I pushed him back up the street to my house.

Pretty soon, I got real good at cutting hair and my basement barber shop started to take off. There were days when I would cut hair for over thirty people. I had a Nintendo game system set up so people could play video games while they waited for a haircut. Moms would bring me their kids and the old men would hang out. The real barber shops in the neighborhood hated me because I was taking business away from them. Everyone liked to come to my basement barbershop and play Nintendo while they waited for a hair cut. Some days I'd be there until midnight cutting hair. On a good week, I'd make five hundred dollars cutting hair.

And I spent all my money on what else – dancing. On the weekends, my sister Nicey and I would blow all my haircut money at the dance clubs. It was a big deal. She and I would always wear matching outfits, like maroon MCM jogging suits. We would always have a dance routine to perform at the club. People would circle around us and we would do our routine. Then we'd each go our separate ways. I never had many dates back then, because I danced so much. Nobody wants to go out with the guy who's all sweaty from dancing. But Nicey and I sure had a whole lot of fun.

It turns out I wasn't the only person who thought about heading back to Logan. Mom had been thinking about it too. And when she and her boyfriend finally split up, she gave him our house-in-da-hood and she headed back to West Virginia, while for some strange reason I decided to stay in Detroit. Ah, the mistakes of the young! It was okay for a while. Mom's boyfriend and I had a good relationship and he let me continue to live in the basement and run my neighborhood barbershop. Soon he had a new girlfriend, and for some strange reason she didn't take too kindly to the son of his old girlfriend living in the basement. Pretty soon I was out on the street – literally living in my car at times.

We experienced a lot of hard times as a family, but I had never been homeless. But, eventually there I was, living in my car – trying to find safe places to sleep at night and going to friends' houses to get an occasional shower. Most of the time, I'd park under the Evergreen Bridge. Pretty soon, my sister caught on to what was happening, and would let me catch some sleep over at her place every now and then. I got a gun and kept it in the console. I am amazed to this day that someone didn't try to carjack me in the middle of the night parked under a bridge somewhere while I was sleeping. God was definitely watching over my young, lost soul.

With my barbershop gone, I needed a job. So I headed down to the mall and got a job at one of the stores stocking shelves. But

I didn't like a job not being around people. So I moved on to a new position at Kenney Shoes selling shoes. I was a pretty good salesman and had a lot of repeat customers. This job was where I also had a bad day where I learned a lot about life.

Late one afternoon, one of my regular customers came by to buy shoes for her kids. When she left, she left her credit card on the counter. It was getting dark and I ran outside to the parking lot to find her. When I came running up to her, she freaked out. She thought I was trying to mug her or something. I felt like dirt. When I gave her back the credit card, she was really embarrassed. Whenever she came back to the store to shop, she'd bring me little gifts and stuff.

Things came to a head for me in Detroit one night when I was hanging out with my buddy Levar. I got home from my latest dead-end job washing cars and we were going to go out. I stopped by a party where he was supposed to be and started looking for him. He was in a heated argument with a couple of guys and I thought it was best for us to just get out of there. We avoided getting into a fight. I should have taken that as an omen for what was going to happen for the rest of the evening. Instead we decided we would cross the river and go over to Canada.

Before we headed over to Canada, we stopped at a little store on the corner of Hubble and Plymouth. The store was in a rough section of town, but no worse than my own neighborhood was, so I always felt fairly safe there. There was a coney island stand across the street. It seemed like no matter what time I pulled into the store, there was always a police officer in a car across the street and cops eating coney islands. So we pulled into the parking lot, jumped out and went inside to get some drinks and snacks.

When we went into the store, the parking lot was empty. When we came back out, a couple of cars had pulled into the far corner and some folks got out of their cars to party. We sat in my car for a few minutes and munched down on our snacks. As we ate, I looked up around the corner and I noticed a panel van going past the street by the parking lot. I didn't think anything about it. But, then, about a minute later, I saw the panel van coming up from the alley behind us. The van parked real tight against my back bumper and two guys jumped out. All of a sudden, I knew this was not going to be good.

The passenger in the panel van ran up to my open driver's side window and stuck a gun in my face. I put my hands up and he pulled back. I thought about trying to go for my own gun in the glove box. Then, I looked down and there was a laser pointer targeted on my chest. The laser pointer was jumping around so I knew he was nervous. I decided to try and play it cool. "Man, don't shoot me. I'm too skinny to take a bullet."

The dude with the gun on me started telling me he wanted my money. Levar began arguing with the driver of the van who was at his window. I had already pulled Levar out of one fight that night, and this was not the place to think about pulling him out of a second one. I was surprised by it myself, but the guy with the gun on me and I began talking. He was trying to get my cash and I was trying to keep him from shooting me. The longer I had him talking, the lighter his grip became on the trigger.

It's funny how calm you can become when someone has a gun pointed at your chest. I just kept talking to the dude and hoping Levar didn't do something stupid to get us shot. It's funny, but all the time this was happening, the people that pulled into the parking lot were still partying, like nothing was happening.

Finally, the dude with the gun on me told me he thought I was cool, but he had to do something to keep us from following them when they left. He told us to get out of the car and he was going to take my car. When I resisted, he laughed. He told me he was not going to do anything to the car and I would find it again in a couple of days in the same condition it was. He forced us out of the car. His buddy jumped in the van. The dude who had been talking to me jumped in my car and sped off.

Like idiots, Levar and I took off running to his house, which was only a block or two away. We thought we were going to jump in his car and try to chase them down. Luckily for us, Levar's car wouldn't start.

About a week later, the police found my car parked on the side street. Just like the dude with the gun had told me, nothing was wrong with car. The keys were on the floor board, the gun was still in the glove box, and the drinks and snacks were still in the front seat.

I had my car back but that was it. I made a decision. It was time for me to leave Detroit. It was not easy for me, especially because I had to leave my friends behind. But I knew if I stayed in Detroit, I would end up dead.

It was time to go home to Logan, West Virginia. It was time to go to Doonieville.

Chapter Six

When I was a kid growing up in Logan, I came up with the idea that one day I wanted to start my own town and call it Doonieville. I used it as a joke my whole life. But even when I'm messing around about it, Doonieville is a real place for me. It was created from my days of exploring the beautiful mountains in West Virginia and refined during the time I was running around the mean streets of Detroit.

When I was growing up, we always took care of each other. For a while, we lived with my grandparents, Flora Lee and Horatio Thomas Paige. There must've been fifteen of us in the house when we lived there. You learn a lot of life lessons with that many people living in one house.

In Logan, I learned my order in the totem pole of my family (which also means your order for the bathroom in the morning). I learned how to ride a bike and climb a tree. I learned I love pork chops and mashed potatoes, but I hate peas. I learned how to make a syrup sandwich when we didn't have much else to eat.

But even more important, at a young age I learned how to stand up and be a man. Many people who grow up the way I did would quit. Logan was the place where I learned to believe in myself and where I became determined to follow my dream.

My ideas about Doonieville got clearer when I lived in Detroit. I saw how people passed judgment on me, even though they had no idea who I was or what my dreams were. That lady in the parking lot outside Kenney Shoes would have to get special permission to live in my city.

That's why Doonieville would be a town in the mountains of West Virginia. It would be a place where the color of a person's skin didn't matter. Coal miners are all black anyway. Everyone would have a job to do, and people would look out for each other. A person's value in Doonieville would not be decided by how much money they have. Instead a person's importance would be determined by how much they helped their fellow man. Kids wouldn't go to bed hungry. Musicians and artists would have as much value as politicians and lawyers.

I used to tell my brothers and sisters that I would create my city on the mountain right across from the little house where we grew up. The streets would actually spell out the name of the city – Doonieville. That way you could see Doonieville when you flew over it in an airplane. It became my version of Utopia.

As an adult, I know the perfect community doesn't exist. But, it would still be cool to see streets spell out the word Doonieville.

After winning *America's Got Talent*, I came pretty close to my definition of Doonieville when the State of West Virginia actually named the street coming into Logan "Landau Lane" during a big ceremony. The impact of that ceremony didn't really hit me until my manager, Burke Allen, told me he was helping his son with homework one night, and "Little Burke" was using the Google Earth™ satellite program for some school project. Google Earth is an online program where you can explore all over the world with the click of a mouse. For the project, they looked at the pyramids in Egypt, the glaciers of Antarctica and the Australian outback. When they looked up Logan, West Virginia, they found "Landau Lane" spelled out on the map. It wasn't Doonieville Lane, but pretty darn close. I can live with that.

Now I understand that Logan, West Virginia is my Doonieville. I already knew that when I left Detroit. And I know that today. So, when I left Detroit and headed to Logan, it was my attempt to get back to a simpler life and to straighten my act out.

One of the other reasons I decided to go back to Logan was that my little brother was running with a bad crowd. I decided it was my role as his big brother to straighten him out. That was a bad call on my part. Once I was back in Logan, I fell into some bad habits I developed in Detroit and started running with my little brother's friends and going down the same bad path.

My life changed for the good when I started spending time with Jennifer. We had known each other as kids. In fact, she actually remembers her dad giving me money to moonwalk around the living room in my Spiderman underwear when we were kids. I started becoming real interested in her, but she made it very clear she was not interested in me unless I straightened up. And so I did.

Jennifer was working at the Bob Evans in Logan waiting on tables and she got me a job there as a bus boy. We started dating and the rest, as they say, is history. Jennifer and I got married on November 25, 2005.

I gave it my best effort to show Jennifer that I was serious about getting my act together. I held a bunch of jobs around Logan. I worked at the restaurant with Jennifer. I started washing cars at a dealership again. I was a telemarketer for a while. I even worked for a time as a flag man on a construction crew for a company owned by Jack Whittaker, the guy who won the huge lottery jackpot. I never met Jack personally until after I won *America's Got Talent* and we both were celebrity waiters at a charity event. He came up and introduced himself to me and told me all the guys on my old road crew were proud of me. That really meant a lot.

When I was back in Logan, Jennifer encouraged me to start singing more. One of the big events in Logan is the annual Arts and Crafts Fair that is held down at the field house. The highlight of the festival is the talent show. I had tried to get into the talent show before, but I guess I didn't look like I fit in. Then in 2003 Debrina Williams from the Chamber of Commerce got me in the show.

I came out and performed "My Way" by Frank Sinatra. I knocked it down and brought down the house. Nobody knew who I was, but everyone in the audience gave me a standing ovation. I won the contest and they gave me a big trophy. Mom still has it in her house along with the picture they had of me in the *Logan Banner* newspaper.

Winning the talent contest suddenly opened up a whole new avenue of performing for me. People started asking me to come and perform at their charity events and parties. It didn't take long for me to get known as someone who could entertain a crowd in Logan. But still, I had trouble finding places to sing.

That's why I had started singing with Top Shelf. I had a dream I could make it as a singer and performer, but I wasn't sure how to get there. The funny thing about singing with Top Shelf was the guys in my band didn't like doing the Frank Sinatra/Dean Martin/Rat Pack stuff. I thought the crooner songs fit in really well with the rhythm and blues format, but they just didn't like it. After all, it was backwoods West Virginia. So I used to go into clubs with them and sing Motown, Southern Rock, Country or pretty much whatever people wanted to hear.

While I loved performing with Top Shelf, I hated playing the clubs—smoke-filled, redneck clubs where we got work. People would smoke a lot at the clubs. We'd be setting up and you could see the smoke start to build. By the time we would get to the stage, the smoke would sometimes be so thick I could barely see the back of the dance floor from my microphone.

Performing in those smoke-filled clubs used to cause me to get real bad sinus infections. The day after we'd perform, I would feel horrible. I'd spend all week trying to get better, and then I'd start it all over again the next weekend. Sometimes my head would be so stopped up, I felt like I was singing in a tunnel.

One of the "big gigs" we got was opening for the Davisson Brothers, a big-time country act, at the Boone County Fair, which is one county over from Logan. It's not at the end of the earth, but I think you can see it from there.

After we set up all the equipment, I was backstage looking out at the audience and I started to get really, really nervous. It became quickly apparent I was the only black face at the whole danged fair. My hands started to sweat as I began to wonder if I was the only black man in all of Boone County. As we prepared to take the stage, I was sure that I would get a bottle thrown at my head or something. I told the band we needed to start with something strong. So we mixed up the set and decided to open with "Ain't Too Proud to Beg" by The Temptations.

I was more than nervous. Hell, I was scared.

But, the second I blurted out "I know you want to leave me, but I refuse to let you go" the audience went nuts. People that had been staring at me started dancing and singing along. All my fears of being in the wrong crowd went out the window. They may have all been a different color, but they dug the music. Just like today, no one expects my voice to come out of me, and when it does, everything changes.

While I'm reminiscing about the "old days," I can't help but mention the annual "We Can" Vaudeville Review in Logan. My attorney pal Bob Noone helped organize this event every year as a benefit for the Children's Home Society. This event is a standard in Logan and is held in this wonderful old converted movie theater in the heart of downtown called the Coalfield Jamboree. The Vaudeville Review always had a little bit of everything on stage – bands, singers, dancers, variety acts – and all the proceeds from the event went to help the kids at the home.

The first time I appeared at the "We Can" Bob Noone got up to introduce me and went on and on about how I had wanted to perform before, but how he hadn't really heard me sing until the Arts & Crafts Festival. Right in front of everybody, he apologized to me for not letting me into the lineup sooner. It took a big man to do that and I never forgot it. After that first show, he kept telling me I was wasting my time singing in Logan and I was destined for bigger and better things.

Bob Noone ended up becoming one of my best friends and biggest supporters in life. I sang at his wedding to his wife, the lovely Beth, and Bob helped me so much after winning *America's Got Talent,* helping me build what I call, "Team Landau." Bob still handles all my legal stuff and I appreciate his support from the beginning so very much.

One year before I hit it big on *America's Got Talent*, Bob asked me to be a part of the show. Even though I was making minimum wage at my day job, I agreed to do it. Many of my friends told me I was nuts and that I should demand to be paid for singing at the Review. Despite all of the negative vibes, Jennifer and I decided that even if we didn't have a whole lot of money, we could give back to the less fortunate by singing for them. I called Bob and told him I'd do the gig.

All the folks at the Review were so appreciative. For me, it was an important lesson I never forgot – giving back matters. Now, at many of my concerts, Team Landau looks for ways to give back to the community where I'm performing. We do a lot of charity gigs that raise a lot of money for good, worthy causes. It's been one of the true blessings in my life.

Now that I'm making a little more than minimum wage, I still try to do the "We Can" Vaudeville Review. A few months after winning *America's Got Talent*, I was booked to play the legendary Ram's Head Live in Annapolis, Maryland. It was really hectic at the time and I didn't realize we booked the show on a date that conflicted with the Review. I was torn up about it. A good friend and big supporter back in Logan, Diana Barnette, sent her private plane up to Maryland in order to get me back in time for the show. When I got to the Coalfield Jamboree, Burke Allen ran to the soundboard, introduced me and I walked out onto the stage like it had all been perfectly timed and planned. No one ever suspected it was a fire drill.

The good part about that Review was Bob Noone's band, Daddy Rabbit, was playing. Bob and I were back on stage together – just like old times. And we brought down the house.

People often ask me why Top Shelf fell apart and I always tell them typical "band drama." The bass player started getting real childish about the gigs we were playing. A couple of times we were in the middle of a set and he just quit playing. Rick Lowe didn't want to fire him because he was the only one that had all the passwords to the Top Shelf website with all the band's music and pictures. The bass player quit and took all our photos, videos and web content with him. Rick wanted to start a new band, but I was done with that scene. It was time for me to move on.

The breakup of Top Shelf led to the whole set of circumstances that led me to the moment in time where I started to take my future into my hands. It led me to the point where I headed to New York to find my fame and fortune.

I made it onto the audition for *America's Got Talent*. Howie was right – my life changed.

Even though I had been singing around Southern West Virginia for years, after the audition was on television the people in Logan started looking at me in a different way. I had about a week before I went to Las Vegas for the next part of the competition. I couldn't go out of the house without everybody waving at me and stopping to wish me good luck. Suddenly, even a trip to the store would take forever.

One night just before I left for Las Vegas, I ran down to the WalMart to get some milk and eggs. Because of everything that happened during the week, I decided to go to the store at 4:00 a.m. to avoid getting caught up with the store's customers. I never knew there were so many people at WalMart at that hour of the morning. It took me four hours to get out of the store. Folks wanted to talk and get a picture and an autograph. And I stopped and talked with each person, smiled for each photo and signed each autograph.

There was this one good old boy, wearing a WVU ball cap and a real heavy West Virginia accent, who pointed his finger at me while shouting: "You him!" He went on to tell me how he'd been working on his pickup truck in the garage when his wife told him to come in and listen to Frank Sinatra. He said, "I went into the kitchen and started washing my hands while listening to the song. When I walked around the corner, I saw you. I told my wife, 'Hell, that ain't Frank Sinatra. That boy's blacker than the ace of spades!'"

I didn't know quite how to respond to that comment. He really didn't mean anything by it, so I just thanked him and went on my way. I tell that story now at all my concerts and people crack up. I take it in stride. That's my hometown of Logan.

When I finally got home, Jennifer was amazed it'd taken me so long just to pick up some groceries. We laughed about how the show had changed our lives. Suddenly, instead of just making it on the televised audition, I was thinking about how to make it to the next episode.

No more trips to WalMart for a while. It was time to get serious. It was time to head to Las Vegas.

Chapter Seven

When I was on the audition for *America's Got Talent*, Piers Morgan asked me if I had ever auditioned for anything before in my life. When I told him no, it was the truth. Twice before I had the opportunity to audition, but each time I froze up.

During the time period when I was working at the Southfield Chrysler Jeep Eagle in Southfield, Michigan, I had my first shot at an audition. I liked to sing as I washed cars and everyone around the lot liked to listen. One of the workers at the store was related to the singer, Big Slab. I loved Big Slab. My friend kept telling Big Slab about how I had a great voice and that I should be singing for a living. One day, Big Slab came through town and my friend got him on the phone for what was kind of like an audition. When I tried to sing into the phone, I froze up. My friend was all over me telling me I'd never get another shot. I knew he was wrong.

My second shot came when Motown was conducting open auditions in Detroit. I sang karaoke at a few clubs and all my friends would come to hear me sing. They convinced me to go to the Motown audition.

I worked up a rendition of "My Girl" by the Temptations and practiced it over and over again. The day came and I was sitting in the waiting room with a bunch of other folks. We all started singing together to warm up our voices. One of the producers came out of a studio, pointed at me and said, "Boy, come on in here and give me some of that."

Once again, I froze. I went into the studio and I couldn't remember the words to "My Girl" – a song I'd been singing all my life. They tried to get me to relax, but I just couldn't do it. Every time I tried to sing "My Girl," the words just weren't there. They told me to go back out into the waiting room and try to calm down. When I walked out of the audition room I just kept walking. I was mad. I had a shot with the producers of Motown and I blew it.

Looking back—I was barely 21 years old. It was my big shot, but God stepped in and said, "No, this one is not for you. It's not your time."

When I headed to Las Vegas for the first episode of *America's Got Talent*, I knew instinctively it was, in fact, my time. The set of circumstances that led to me applying for the show convinced me of that. I went to Vegas with confidence.

The episode shot in Las Vegas turned out to be the hardest week of the show. It was filmed in an empty studio rather than in front of a live audience. An audience inspires me. I love to sing for people, not a television camera. What was really bad was Jennifer was not with me. This was the one week of the show when I was on my own. I didn't like that. Jennifer had been my rock and foundation for the audition, and I wanted her to be there with me in Vegas.

One thing that was cool about the week in Vegas was getting to spend a lot of time with the producer I met that previous year. Mike Farrell and I really bonded that week in Las Vegas. He kept telling me I was the "star of the show" and I was going to be the "one to beat." He really did a lot for my confidence. If you go back and check the clips of the show, Mike is the guy playing piano when I sang "Kick in the Head."

The bad part about the show in Vegas was someone I developed a friendship with, singer Cindy Cheyne, got cut. Cindy had a Ph.D. in music and sang opera. She had a fantastic voice. I was backstage watching the monitors while she was singing, and I remember her stumbling a bit during the song. I think because we were not in front of an audience, she was a bit nervous. When the judges ripped her, I started to freak out. My confidence slipped a bit. Cindy was a music teacher with creds and I was just a guy from Logan, West Virginia.

I remember deciding at that moment to just let go. I determined that God brought me to that precise point for a reason, and it was simply time to let Him step in. I decided to stop trying to do too much and let His will be done. I started accepting the moment for what it was. In the end, my performances were much better because of that decision. That was also the moment I decided to stop rehearsing for each episode. I knew the music and was confident in my abilities. It was time to let God direct me through each show. He got me this far, He could surely get me to the finish line.

The strategy worked. I felt a huge relief when I sang for the judges in Las Vegas. "Kick in the Head" flowed from me. I messed up the song a bit at the end. I didn't get all of my emotion into the final note. But, when I finished, I knew I was on my way to Hollywood.

"...because Landau is the man..."
—Actor Robbie Amell, *Cheaper By the Dozen 2,*
television's *Scooby-Doo! The Mystery Begins* and
Scooby-Doo! Curse of the Lake Monster and
Nickelodeon's *True Jackson, VP*

Chapter Eight

Hollywood had a whole different feel to it. In each episode, I was in front of a live audience. That was really important to me. Like I said before, I love singing to the audience. If you watched any of the episodes, you may have noticed I tended to not look at the television camera too much. That is because I was interacting with the audience.

When we got to Hollywood, for Jennifer and me, it was all business. For the first time in my life, I felt like I was on the verge of living my dream. I did not want to do anything to mess it up. A lot of the other people on the show went to all the Hollywood parties and places to get the "red carpet" treatment. I had a strong feeling God put me there to do a job, and it was my job to remain focused on the competition.

What was weird for me was that people in Hollywood started recognizing me. One day Jennifer and I were walking down the street and a car slammed on its brakes. The car stopped so fast another car smacked into it from behind. Jennifer and I looked at each other kind of shocked because we had just seen an accident. The driver of the car that stopped jumped out of his car, started pointing at me shouting, "Black Frank Sinatra! Black Frank Sinatra!" The lady in the car behind him was real upset. But the driver of the first car pulled out his cell phone and started snapping pictures of Jennifer and me.

Another time, Jennifer and I were having lunch at Chipotle. We were sitting in the front window just eating and watching people walk down Sunset Boulevard. I looked up through the window and noticed a couple looking at Jennifer and me. The guy was pointing and talking real fast. It took a minute, but I suddenly realized it was actor Robbie Amell and his girlfriend, Italia Ricci. I remember Robbie from when he played the role of Fred in the Scooby-Doo movies and the kid's TV show, *True Jackson*.

Robbie walked over to the window where we were sitting, and asked real slow if I was Landau. I guess he wanted me to read his lips from inside the restaurant. Well, I did. So, I laughed and nodded my head. Jennifer and I wandered outside and struck up a conversation with them. It turns out they were big fans of *America's Got Talent* and really enjoyed my performances. Robbie invited Jennifer and me to his house to play basketball, which was great. I hadn't shot any hoops for weeks. The ability to go to Robbie's house and play some basketball was a great stress reliever for me. Jennifer and I started hanging out there a lot.

One night, when we were sitting on the deck at Robbie's house, I looked towards the mountains and saw a double rainbow. That was the second time in my journey I had seen a double rainbow. The first time was the day I applied to be a contestant on *America's Got Talent*. I'm sure I had seen one before, but I really couldn't remember when. The one I saw in Logan that day really made an impression on me. It was like God was telling me it was the right thing to do. Now, here I was in Hollywood and there was another double rainbow off in the distance.

And that wasn't the last time I'd see a double rainbow. After I won, they held a parade for me back in Logan. It was raining that day and, sure enough, as we meandered our way through the streets of Logan, there was another double rainbow. Looking back, it was more than a coincidence. I really believe it was a sign. Three double rainbows to win season six of *America's Got Talent*.

Jennifer and I also loved just walking around the city. One day, I convinced Snap-Boogie to take a walk with Jennifer and me down the Sunset Strip. Snap was one of the other contestants on *America's Got Talent*. I took Snap under my wing because he was a dancer like I had been as a kid. He was also one of the young kids on the show that called me Uncle Doonie. Anyway, we were out walking around when Snap had to use the restroom real bad. A gas station wouldn't let us in, so I sent Snap into a café a few doors away. Jennifer and I were waiting outside of the place when I noticed a guy sitting in a chair on the end of the porch. It was Heavy D.

I went nuts and started singing "We Got Our Own Thing," one of his songs from his platinum CD, *Big Tyme*. He recognized me from the show and started smiling at my rendition of his song. I told him how my sister and I had made up dance routines to his songs. It turned out the café was owned by one of Heavy D's friends and he hung out there all the time. He laughed when Snap came out and didn't know who he was. "He's too young," he said.

Heavy D told me he voted for me on *America's Got Talent* and then gave me some advice on stardom. "Watch yourself," he warned. "You're about to lose a lot of friends and relatives." He paused a second and added, "And sign all your own checks." He gave me his cell phone number and told me to call him when the show was over. I never got the chance. A month later, Heavy D died from heart disease.

A lot of folks gave me similar advice. One day Obba Babatunde called our hotel room. When he asked if I knew who he was, I blurted out, "You're Berry Gordy!" Obba had played the role of Berry Gordy, Jr. in *The Temptations*, one of my favorite movies of all time. I was amazed he was calling me. "Youngblood," he said, "you just keep doin' what you've been doin'. Just watch your back."

A lot of people ask me how the songs were chosen for each episode. One cool thing about *America's Got Talent* is that, except for the celebrity duet, each performer gets to choose the songs they sing for every episode. My songs all reflected my mood at the time. When I sang, "I've Got the World on a String," it was how I felt. I sang "Kick Out of You" because I was having so much fun with the audience. I sang "I've Got You Under My Skin," to let everyone watching know I was just like them.

The producers wanted me to sing "My Way" earlier, but I was saving that one for last. For me, there was no question – "My Way" was my closer.

The episodes all went well, except for the one where they added dancers to my show. I quit rehearsing after Las Vegas. I knew all the songs by heart and was confident I could knock them down.

Then the producers of *America's Got Talent* came to me and requested I add dancers to one of my songs. I was totally opposed. I mean, it was my butt on the line. If one of the dancers screwed up, it would affect my performance (and more importantly – my votes). But somehow I let them talk me into it. Rehearsal was horrible. I couldn't get the spin right and even had the folks in wardrobe widen the buttonhole on my jacket so I could make my jacket fly open. When we started the song, my hands were sweating like mad. Like before, I just put everything out of my mind and tried to concentrate on the moment. I hit the spin and the jacket flew open right on cue.

The real cool thing about Hollywood was my kids all got to come out and see me perform. They heard me sing around the house and at church, but they had never seen me sing in front of a live audience. Michael, Marcus, Morgan and Kyra all got to come out. After one of the shows, they got to be on television. That was big for all of their friends back home.

All my life I told my kids to dream big. And there they were, right by my side as I followed my dream.

Chapter Nine

The last week of the show was a blessing and a curse. I had family come in from all over the country – my mom, my brothers and sisters, and all my kids. But all the confusion of having them around added to the stress of the final couple of performances.

When I first headed out to be on *America's Got Talent*, Jennifer's mom asked me who I would like to do my duet with. From the very beginning, I said I wanted to sing with Miss Patti LaBelle. When we got to that point in the production of the show, the producers asked me for a list of who I wanted perform with. When I gave them a list of one – Patti LaBelle – they said they would make contact with her, but I should probably come up with a couple of other names. They didn't think Patti would want to sing with me.

The day before the duets show, the producers gave me the sheet music to "You're All I Need to Get By" by Ashford and Simpson. I knew the song and I started going over my part in a rehearsal room. I had been watching as others paired up with their celebrities. I still had no idea who I was going to be singing with.

As it turns out, Patti LaBelle was a fan of *America's Got Talent*. Even more amazing was that she had been following my appearances on the show. When the producers called her to perform with me, she jumped at the chance.

They called me out of my room and the first person I saw was Queen Latifah, so I thought I was going to be singing with her. I shouted out, "Queen Latifah in the house." She laughed and said, "Baby, come give Queen Latifah a hug."

When Patti came walking up, I lost my mind. It dawned on me I wasn't singing with Queen Latifah, but Patti LaBelle. I was overcome with the fact I was going to perform with one of the greatest voices to ever grace a stage. I started crying. Jennifer was in tears. Patti looked at me and said, "You're 37. I'm 67. We're gonna rock." Then she said a prayer for me. It was incredible.

We only rehearsed for about fifteen minutes and knocked it down.

After our rehearsal, Patti took us to Pink's Famous Hot Dogs in Los Angeles for dinner. She wanted me to order some exotic hot dog, but I just stuck with the basics. She walked me around to every table and introduced me to everyone. She made each person promise to watch the show the next night and vote for me. When she took us back to our hotel in her limousine, she gave me some advice. "Don't let it go to your head and watch out for the snakes," she said. Then she looked at Jennifer. "And keep your wife by your side."

The next day, Patti lived up to her promise. WE ROCKED.

When she came out, she started vamping while the orchestra was playing the verse she planned to sing. "Hey, Landau," she was singing. I was following the band and realized we were about to hit the bridge of the song. When I pointed up, she switched over to the regular lyrics in the song. And together, we brought down the house.

What was really cool was that when we finished singing, Patti disappeared from the stage. She wanted me to have the spotlight. By the time I finished with my interview with Nick Cannon, she was gone.

I went back to the hotel that night thinking, for the first time, I really did have a chance to win.

Growing up in a family that liked to party had its advantages. I learned how to sing and dance at a very early age. When Jennifer and I got back to the room the party was in full swing. But, this was not the night I needed to be around a party. A bunch of my family was staying in my room, too. It took forever (with a little help from hotel security) to get everyone to go to sleep. Jennifer and I ended up sharing our bed with a couple of nephews and nieces. I didn't get any sleep the night before the final show.

The next morning, I fell asleep on the shuttle ride to the studio.

On the day of a show, the performers spend a lot of time in wardrobe, makeup and shooting B-roll. I must have looked like death when I got to the studio because everyone left me alone. I went to the Green Room, curled up on the couch, and went to sleep. I heard later a couple of the acts complained I was sleeping in the Green Room. Sorry guys, but I was tired.

As the final show was progressing, I just kept trying to clear my mind. "My Way" is one of my favorite songs because it speaks to what I had been through in my life. When I got to the stage to sing it—all the emotions of thirty-six years of hard-livin' were flowing through my veins. I put it all out there.

Waiting for the final tally, I started to get real nervous.

Then they said my name. I remember just putting my head down into my hands and wondering if I was dreaming. "Did they really just say my name?"

"Joining Team Landau was like running off to join the circus."

—Burke Allen, Manager, Team Landau

Chapter Ten

Once I won *America's Got Talent*, everything started happening real quick. I stayed up most of the night at the post show celebrations. The next morning I did a whole bunch of interviews. It felt like I hadn't slept in days (and to some degree I hadn't). Everybody wanted to celebrate, but all I wanted to do was get back to Logan and go to sleep.

But before I went home, I had to go to New York City. The folks at Sony's Columbia Records wanted to meet with me. Everybody thought that part of the prize for winning *America's Got Talent* was that I got a recording deal with Columbia Records. That wasn't quite true. They had the option to sign me, but it wasn't a done deal. So Jennifer and I headed back to the Big Apple, the place where it all started, to see and meet with their executives.

Now while the show had been going on, my friend Bob Noone had been getting a lot of requests for interviews. I didn't know it at the time, but Bob had been using Burke Allen to handle the press for him. Burke is part of the extended Logan family, having grown up with Bob, but he had his own public relations firm in Northern Virginia just across the Potomac River from Washington, D.C. Since Bob had been handling all of my legal work, I called and asked him if he would come to New York with us to meet with all the record executives. He said he would try, and Jennifer and I got ready to head to New York.

Unbeknownst to me, Bob figured out he had a conflict and could not make it to New York City. So he picked up the phone and called Burke Allen and asked him to meet Jennifer and me at our hotel. Poor guy, one minute he was outside doing some yard work with his wife and the next minute he was on a train with just an overnight bag headed to New York City.

Burke got to the hotel about the same time we did, and it was a good thing, too. Sony had taken care of the room for us but we still needed a credit card to check in. The hotel said they needed it for incidentals. Until a couple of nights before, I didn't have credit, let alone a credit card. It was really messed up and the hotel was not going to let us check in without a credit card. I actually thought we were going to have to sleep on a bench at the bus station before our meeting. Thankfully, that's when Burke Allen walked into our lives. He put down his own credit card and got us into our rooms.

It was late – about 1:00 a.m. – but all three of us were hungry. We went out to get some dinner, which you can do in Manhattan, even on a Sunday night at 1:00 a.m. I think at first Burke was a little taken aback when I asked him to join hands with Jennifer and me so we could say grace. He told me later that was one of the things that impressed him with our first meeting.

Monday morning we headed out to the Sony Building and Columbia Records, and man was I glad that Burke was there with us. We went up to the 20th floor and there were a bunch of folks waiting for us in a conference room. As they introduced themselves, I really didn't know who they were, but Burke sure knew the names of several of them. Steve Tyrell, who had won a couple of Grammy Awards working with people like Rod Stewart and Diana Ross and produced numerous hit albums of his own was there. John Deolp (producer of most of Celine Dion's biggest hits and Columbia's A&R guy) and legendary British artist manager Peter Rudge (who worked with the Rolling Stones, The Who and Lynyrd Skynyrd) were also in the room.

I was told that Columbia was under no obligation to produce me. There were no guarantees. But Burke figured out quickly that, because of who was in the room, it was apparent they wanted to produce my record. Of course, I'm glad he didn't tell me that, or I would have been very nervous. My hands would've really been sweating. It was really cool to be in the place where Frank Sinatra,

Tony Bennett, Billy Joel, Bruce Springsteen, Adele and Beyonce and more recorded. We all hit it off immediately and pretty soon Steve Tyrell and I were singing songs together and starting to plan for him to produce the album, and Peter and Burke talked about co-managing the launch of my new career.

Noon time came and we headed up to the penthouse dining room to have lunch with Steve Barnett, the head of Sony Music. It was pretty high brow. There were guys in white gloves serving caviar. At one point, Burke leaned over and whispered in my ear, "Hey man, I don't think we're in Kansas any more."

Well, they made us an offer and asked that I stick around for an extra day or so to cut some tracks and do some publicity. I was dog tired and wanted badly to get back to Logan, but I agreed. So, Steve Tyrell and I headed to the studio, while Jennifer got to know Burke a bit better. It was becoming apparent to us that we couldn't do all of this by ourselves. Burke was originally from Logan and a friend of Bob's, which meant a lot with all the new people coming into our lives. Our families knew each other back in West Virginia, and Burke seemed to know someone in music and media everywhere we went. Jennifer and I asked him to join the team. Burke agreed and booked us all a flight back to Logan. He went with us to do an appearance on Anderson Cooper's TV show—then back into the recording studio at Times Square for more work with Steve, Peter and arranger Bob Mann.

We booked the earliest flight we could get out of LaGuardia Wednesday morning at 6:00 a.m. to get back to Logan. We got to the airport in plenty of time, but it was wild. People were recognizing me and Jennifer from the show, and all kinds of folks were asking for pictures and autographs. We had to make a connection in Charlotte and nearly missed it because a mob of people stopped us as we made our way from gate to gate. Burke learned then that everything we planned to do would take a bit longer than it should, because I would always stop to sign autographs and take pictures.

It got even wilder. I started signing autographs as soon as we walked through the gate at Yeager Airport in Charleston. When

Burke went to pick up our rental car to get us to Logan, instead of the usual compact, the guy at the counter threw us the keys to a brand new, tricked out Dodge Charger and said, "Enjoy it on us…and welcome home!" On the 50 minute drive home, people had put up billboards all along Corridor "G" from Charleston to Logan welcoming us home and congratulating me on my *America's Got Talent* win. Even the West Virginia state highway department got in on the act. They put out messages on all their blinking highway signs saying how proud the state was of what we had done.

Everybody back in Logan followed the show very closely. People had viewing parties every week. A lot of folks sent me telegrams, emails and texts wishing me good luck. The last night of the show, they set up a big viewing party at the local cinema there, owned by my pal, Diana Barnette, so everybody could come down and watch *America's Got Talent* together. The Chamber of Commerce was really into it and all the local TV stations covered the story

Before we got back to Logan, Burke called Dave Allen, the morning personality from the local radio station in town, WVOW (which stands for the Wonderful Voice of West Virginia). Dave is a great guy, and he had been a big supporter of me way before my appearance on *America's Got Talent*. When I was a highway flagman, I used to stop traffic so Dave could turn up the hill to his driveway; that's the kind of town we're from. Logan only has about 3,000 residents. Dave said there was easily twice that many already in Logan, and they expected 10,000 people by the end of the day, including the Governor. Even though it was raining, people were already starting to line up for the parade, and TV, radio and print journalists from all over were in town to cover the welcome home celebration.

Burke dropped us off at my mother-in-law Miss Idella's house so Jennifer and I could changes clothes and rest for a few hours before the parade. It had been less than a week since I won the contest, and we had barely slept. We were running on pure adrenaline. While we grabbed an all too-short nap, Burke ran up to the

Walmart to get some clothes. The poor guy had come to New York City four days earlier with only an overnight bag and hadn't been home since. When Dave Allen told him he was going to meet with the Governor of West Virginia, he figured he ought to have on a fresh change of clothes. As it turned out, he wouldn't get home for another two weeks. He said it was like running off to join the circus.

We all headed up to the high school where the parade started and slipped into the band room to get ready and say hi to the Governor and a few other guests. At the time it was still raining. Just as they came to get me and Jennifer and put us in the back of a convertible, the rain quit. When we sat in the back of the car, someone pointed up behind me at the double rainbow in the sky. As we tried to pull out, there was a big push of people against the car. Burke and Dave from the radio station started walking alongside the car with us so the car could get through and to help keep people from getting hurt. I started laughing because they looked like my low-rent Secret Service agents leading the car through the streets of Logan.

As we drove through the town, people were cheering and crying and singing. Jennifer cried the whole way through. Main and Stratton Street in downtown Logan are very narrow and people were standing 15 deep on both sides. I clearly remember Debra Shaw standing on the side of one street singing, "Who did it?"

I sang back: "God did it."

"Who did it?"

"God did it."

When we got back to the high school we went to the band room to get ready for the ceremony at the field house. The Logan Memorial Field House holds about 4,000 people. It was estimated there were at least 7,000 people there that day. The lights were out and Bob Noone's band, Daddy Rabbit, started playing. We walked out and thousands of flashbulbs started going off. It was a very emotional moment for me to be back HOME with so many of the people who believed in me during the journey. You could feel the love in the room and I can't tell you how many times I broke down and cried during the ceremony. It was very surreal. I felt like I was an actor playing myself in a movie about my life.

The Chamber of Commerce gave me an award. My Congressman, Nick Rahall, was there to congratulate me. And Mayor Serafino Nolletti, whose family owned City Bakery for almost 100 years, read a proclamation making it Landau Day in Logan.

When Governor Earl Ray Tomblin and the First Lady got to the podium, I kind of lost it. Governor Tomblin is also from Logan County and his wife, the First Lady, used to be a big time TV news anchor in the Charleston market, and was now the president of the local college. Over the last several months, the Governor ended every speech he gave as governor by saying "Vote for Landau." When he read the proclamation on behalf of the people of West Virginia, I looked down and noticed my hands were starting to shake. I closed my eyes trying to fight back the tears. I was physically and emotionally drained.

When it was my turn to talk, I tried to thank all the people who had been so special to us over the journey. I was so tired I don't remember too much of what I said, and I'm sure I left a lot of people off the list. But at the end, I looked to my left and there was the one person who made it all happen – Jennifer. She had been the one who was with me every step of the way. She is the one who believed in me when no one else did. I pointed at Jennifer and announced to everyone, "That's my girl."

The crowd went nuts! Then, my buddy Bob and the Daddy Rabbit band on the stage behind us started playing that famous bass line to "My Girl" by the Temptations. I pulled the microphone from the holder on the podium and walked over to where Jennifer was sitting and serenaded her with "My Girl." She cried a river, and the whole audience went crazy. I tried to stay and sign as many autographs as I could, but it was impossible…every one of those 7,000 folks wanted and deserved one! Finally, the local police department thought it was getting too out of hand and they hustled us out the back door.

Somehow, we made it to a small reception at Bob Noone's office that he set up for my family and closest friends. Burke couldn't do it—he went to a hotel and collapsed before even making it to the reception. After a couple of hours, Jennifer and I went home to Miss Idella's and literally slept for a day and a half. I swear I didn't get out of bed for nearly 2 days.

But I couldn't rest for long; I was getting ready to hop on a plane to Houston, Texas, on Sunday to start recording my vocals for the CD when I got a request to sing the National Anthem at a West Virginia University football game that Saturday. I love the Mountaineers, and I really wanted to do it, but the logistics just weren't going to work out. So, my new friends Freddie and Mitzi Rick sent their private plane to Logan and a long road trip up to Morgantown turned into a 22 minute jaunt over the mountain for a super secret sound check in the stadium. Another first—a private jet ride. Check that off the list.

The University had been real protective about the identity of the "surprise guest" who was going to be singing the Anthem. That didn't last too long. Since I was going to be singing in front of 70,000 people, I wanted to rehearse. I heard it was hard to sing in big stadiums because of the crowd noise and bounce back. We slipped into the stadium in a black SUV with a police escort. I stood at the 50 yard line and sang the National Anthem a couple of times.

When I finished it the second or third time, my manager Burke Allen got a cell phone call from the parent of a student at WVU who said their daughter could hear me in her dorm room. So I started singing her name, "Shauna O'Briant, This is Landau." By the time I finished, everyone in Morgantown knew I was in the house. I practiced another time and was ready. When I was done, legendary WVU coach Don Nehlen and his wife, who had been watching me practice, came over and congratulated me on my victory.

Since that day, I've sung the National Anthem at several more sporting events, including at Madison Square Garden for ESPN and at Marshall University games. I sang it again at the Governor's inauguration, and at the dedication of the Veteran's Administration Hospital Women's Health Center. It's a hard song to sing, and people often compliment me on the way I sing it. I get frustrated when a performer tries to over sing the National Anthem. It's not a song I think you should try to "own" or showboat on. I always let the song carry itself and try to sing it in a respectful way – almost like a prayer.

Of course, not everyone likes it when I sing the National Anthem. I'm not a good luck charm for the home team. As of the date of this book, every time I sing the National Anthem at a sporting event, the home team loses. The Mountaineers lost the game when I sang it and so did the Marshall Thundering Herd. Professional teams haven't fared any better. Just ask the Oklahoma City Thunder or the Miami Heat. They all lost when I sang at their games. I need to get on a winning streak!

Anyway, when I finished meeting everyone at WVU, we headed back to Logan. I wasn't home for long. Within a couple of hours, I was on my way to Houston and the Wire Roads studio, and Burke, Bob and Jennifer were on their way to Los Angeles to start building what would become "Team Landau."

Chapter Eleven

I wasn't quite sure what to expect from a professional recording session. I had won a TV reality show, and I didn't know if the folks at Sony Music were going to take it seriously or treat the recording as just one degree above recording on my eight-track in my bedroom closet. The more I learned about Steve Tyrell, the more I knew this was going to be a serious session.

Steve decided I should do the vocals in Texas rather than LA in order to avoid all the media while laying down the vocal tracks.

Recording sessions were much harder than the television show. For *America's Got Talent,* I just went out and performed. In the studio, they wanted me to sing every song at least ten times. Then they would make me sing each line to each song individually. I must've done each individual line to each song a dozen or more times. Each time I finished a line, the engineer would say: "Perfect. Do it again."

From Houston, we headed straight to LA to do a photo shoot for the album cover, to meet the musicians for the album and to shoot the videos that would go along with the release.

I really enjoyed being in LA with Steve Tyrell, who is one of the biggest names in the business. The list of people he's collaborated with is a "who's who" of the music industry – Diana Ross, Burt Bacharach, Stevie Wonder, Smokey Robinson, Aaron Neville, Ray Charles, to name just a few. I don't mean to drop names, but this boy had some serious creds. The dude has Grammys on his book shelf.

That's not to say Steve and I didn't have a few artistic differences. One night he had Jennifer, Burke and me over to his home studio. He lives in this beautiful home with a great recording studio right in the living room of his house. It's a lot more high tech than the microphone that used to be hanging from the ceiling of my closet back in Logan. He had me start laying down more vocal tracks. I thought I already laid down tracks that were as good as I can do, but he wanted more. I was tired from the whirlwind of events following the show and he was tired from trying to rush the CD to stores. After telling me to sing one particular song "one more time," I snapped and walked out. By the time we got to our hotel he called and apologized for pushing me too hard and I apologized for being … well … grumpy.

We got over that drama and, after the release of the CD, we even did a couple of gigs together. I give Steve lots of credit for turning out a fantastic album in record time; less than two months after I won America's Got Talent, my debut album "That's Life" was in stores everywhere.

Other than that one little dust up, the recording process was a huge success. Steve Tyrell and the Columbia folks booked our final sessions, where I sang with the whole orchestra at the legendary Capitol Records studio in Hollywood. He hired an incredible group of engineers and musicians, several of whom had actually played with Frank Sinatra himself. At first, I thought that would be awkward – I think they did, too. But once I started singing, they knew we were going to have some fun. Steve was looking for a new sound. He didn't want it to seem like I was impersonating the Rat Pack. After one session, one of the older musicians came up and told me he had more fun playing for me than Sinatra."You took us to another level," he said.

I was truly touched, but I told him: "Man, Frank was The Man. Frank was Frank. Dino was Dino. And Nat was Nat."

He smiled and softly said, "And Landau is Landau, baby."

They planned for a couple weeks of recording time, I guess thinking they were dealing with some country bumpkin from West

Virginia. I laid down my audio tracks in just three days. We shot the videos at the same time. Add another couple of days for photos and publicity and we were packaged and ready to go back east in just eight days. That took everyone (but me) by surprise.

Even though we knocked the CD out very quickly, I still took time to take it all in. One day after finishing up a session, everyone but me and my manager Burke left the studio. It was just the two of us in the room. I must have had a funny look on my face. "What's wrong?" he asked.

"Nothing man," I replied as I looked around the walls. "This is Capitol Records, man." You could feel Sinatra's presence in the room. "This is where Frank did it. It's like walking on hallowed ground."

My CD, "That's Life," was released November 21st, just before Thanksgiving. The song order was perfect:

Ain't That a Kick in the Head
Night and Day
Witchcraft
Something Stupid (featuring Judith Hill)
That's Life
I've Got You Under My Skin
Baby It's Cold Outside (featuring Judith Hill)
I've Got the World on a String
I Get a Kick Out of You
Fly Me to the Moon
My Way

John Doelp from the label said "That's Life" was the quickest release of a high quality product he had ever been involved with. We all worked real hard to get there—and all of the hard work paid off. The CD debuted at #1 on the jazz charts and #38 on the pop charts. I was proud that West Virginia led all other markets in the country in sales. I ended up selling so many CDs at Walmarts in the state, they couldn't keep them in stock. I got invited to

Bentonville, Arkansas to perform at Walmart's big Christmas corporate meeting. I was happy to go out and thank those folks for all they had done to help us succeed.

When I got back to West Virginia, we had to put a great band together and do it fast. Burke was getting more requests for dates than there were available days. And I had been spending all my time on the recording sessions.

Then this guy named Jeff Flanagan called us. Jeff had a big band over in Charleston. Since his band was already playing some of the crooner music, it was the perfect fit. Jeff was great, and he spent a lot of time teaching me the history behind the songs I was performing. He had an ear for a lot of different types of music. I told Jeff and Burke I only had one big condition – I wanted to use as many local musicians as possible. West Virginia had been great to me and I wanted to repay the favor – call it my version of Affirmative Action for West Virginia.

The cool thing about the band we put together is the quality of the performers and the depth we have at each instrument. The size of the group varies depending on the size of the venue and the budget for each gig. I was amazed at how much strong local talent we found. The guys in the band are college music professors and professional musicians who have played for people like Sinatra, Buddy Rich and Tom Jones. We even have the head of the West Virginia Golf Association on drums – just in case I decide to take up golf. As if there's time for that these days.

We only had one real rehearsal together before we actually performed. These fantastic players added so much depth to the songs. Now they are like my family; we've played all over the U.S. and even overseas together.

We've played some great shows, but a couple stand out in my mind–Caesar's Palace in Las Vegas, the legendary Apollo Theatre in Harlem, the Clay Center in Charleston and The Greenbrier.

Part of the prize for winning *America's Got Talent* was headlining a gig at Caesar's Palace featuring a whole bunch of talent from the show. Also on the bill with me were The Silhouettes, magician Landon Swank, singer/pianist Anna Graceman, the band Pop Lyfe, dancers Fighting Gravity and Jack Vigund (winner of *Australia's Got Talent*). It was humbling to be back to a place where months earlier we were wishing and hoping, and now we were living out the dream. Instead of walking through the door of Caesar's Palace, I was flying through with a rocket strapped to my back.

For me, it was really special to be singing Sinatra in the town that Sinatra put on the map. The director of the show was Harry Sandlin, a real pro who worked with all the big talent of the past thirty years, from James Taylor to Van Halen. We had a bunch of rehearsals and he was a perfectionist about how it would be executed. Harry came up with the idea of me walking through the audience while singing "That's Life," something we still use in our shows.

I really enjoyed spending a lot of time with Jerry Springer, the emcee for our show and a former host of *America's Got Talent*. He was a nice guy and really, really funny. The last night of the show, Jerry was going to be on stage as I performed "My Way" and we traded off verses with him doing his best Elvis impersonation.

We sold out Caesar's Palace all three nights. Part of the sellout was compliments of Diana Barnette, the owner of the Cinema 8 back in Logan that held the viewing parties for my *America's Got Talent* run. Diana, Joe Raymond, our buddy from the local bank, and what seemed like dozens of folks from West Virginia all came to Vegas the weekend I played there. Even my old boss at the car lot, Mike Ferrell came! Somebody bought out a huge penthouse at Bally's across the street from Caesar's Palace and filled it up with our friends. A whole bunch of folks from the Logan Chamber of Commerce including Chamber head, Debrina Williams, were there, too. I think they all had a good time. We got to spend some time with the folks from Logan who were there for us from the beginning. But Jennifer and I were so busy, we never got the chance to see any other shows on the famous Vegas strip besides our own!

It was sad to say goodbye to all of the people I performed with on *America's Got Talent*. I knew after the show at Caesar's Palace I was probably never going to see most of them again. We took a whole bunch of pictures and gave lots of hugs. Still, instead of going to a wrap party with the adults, Jennifer and I joined the tween girls from The Silhouettes for ice cream. It was a blast. We were all sitting on the patio of a place called Serendippity talking about our experiences on the show, laughing, cutting up, and taking in all the glamour of the Vegas strip (with ice cream cones).

The gig at The Apollo in Harlem was cool because … well … it's THE APOLLO. I was given the opportunity to be the Celebrity Special Guest during Apollo's famous Amateur Night and, I have to admit, I did that gig for me. I loved being there. I was on the same stage that once featured the likes of Michael Jackson and James Brown. There is a place backstage where Billie Holiday carved her name into the wall.

I got a big surprise at the Apollo when my kids showed up to watch me perform. Their grandfather flew them up so they could see their dad's name on the marquee at The Apollo. That was really special.

I was worried about the audience at the Apollo. They are known to be a pretty rough crowd. If they don't like you, they will get pretty rowdy. I was really excited when they gave me a standing ovation at the end of the night. I thought the crowd would be all black. But it wasn't. The crowd was the greatest mix I'd ever seen. I told my kids it looked like a bag of Skittles and M&Ms – all colors mixed together.

After the show at the Apollo, we went across the street and celebrated with dinner at a local soul food restaurant. At a lot of the places we performed, Jennifer and I would be some of the few black folks in the crowd. Now at this restaurant in Harlem, it was my manager Burke Allen's white face who stood out—it was cool though…he ate with the family…he's one of us.

My three favorite places to play back home in West Virginia are The Greenbrier Resort, the Clay Center in Charleston and the

Coalfield Jamboree in my hometown of Logan. I was amazed how unique each one is. We had requests from all over the state of West Virginia to come play, and I discovered there are a lot of wonderful music venues all over the Mountain State. I never knew we had such beautiful performance venues scattered across West Virginia.

When I'm at those places, I'm performing in front of my homies – my fellow Mountaineers. Every concert at those venues is like a big family reunion with people I'd never met before. You have to be from here to understand the bond that I feel with West Virginia audiences. During *America's Got Talent*, I performed in the center of Hollywood and I'd still rather be in front of my home folks. West Virginians are tough folk. We've spit in the eye of adversity and dared it to flinch.

The cool thing about the performance at the Clay Center—a new state-of-the-art Performing Arts Center in the heart of the capital city of Charleston—was how it came about. The folks there contacted us about doing a show for Christmas immediately after I won *America's Got Talent*. Tickets went on sale and they sold out literally within minutes. So they added a second show. There were stories of lines of cars a mile long trying to get to the box office. The second concert sold out just as fast, crashing their internet sales portal. A third show was added in December 2011, and it sold out, too! We've now done five shows at the Clay Center and each one has been a sellout.

The Greenbrier in White Sulphur Springs, West Virginia is unlike any place in the world. I drove up to the front gate to a little house that had a security guard in it. The guy found my name on the list and we headed up a road to the huge white building that looks like the White House, only bigger. A guy in a top hat and tails came out and took my luggage and when he asked for my car keys I asked if I was going to get them back. He thought I was making a joke. I was serious. The Greenbrier has played host to Presidents, Heads of State, and now for several times…Team Landau.

The Coalfield Jamboree in Logan will always be special. It's an old vaudeville theatre that was converted into a movie theatre, and then back to a live performance venue in the late 1990s. It seats about 1,100 people and usually brings in country, gospel and oldies shows. I did lots of charity appearances there for the Children's Home Society of West Virginia and the Chamber of Commerce way before I was on *America's Got Talent*. After I won, they held a Logan Loves Landau welcome home concert just before Valentine's Day. It was the first sellout they'd had there in over 10 years! The show was loud and rowdy. I had lots of my and Jennifer's family there. Man, that was fun!

One trip I'll never forget is when we performed on Veteran's Day for our military troops in Germany. What an unbelievable honor. But when I was asked to do it, I was a bit leery. First off, Jennifer and I had never been out of the country before. Congressman Rahall took care of that for us. We had been on the road non-stop and unable to get our papers together. So my manager Burke asked the Congressman's staffer Robby Queen if he could help. Robby made special arrangements for us at the federal courthouse in Elkins, WV to stop by the day I performed there at the Mountain State Forest Festival. They helped us get all the paperwork straight.

The other issue with the Germany gig was it didn't pay anything except a small per diem for expenses. I felt like I owed it to the troops who were serving. I was totally cool with doing it for free. But I wasn't sure I could ask my band members to do it for nothing. I should have known better. They jumped at the chance. So, after a long layover at the USO Lounge at Dulles airport in Washington, D.C. where Burke's wife fixed us all a great dinner—Jennifer, Burke, the band members, our ace sound man John Griffiths and I got on a plane and headed to Germany.

It turns out that *America's Got Talent* was broadcast in Germany. Who knew? I'd walk down the street in Munich or Stuttgart and people would point at me and say with a real heavy accent, "Landau Eugene Murphy, Jr." I had no idea what they said after that. I just smiled and nodded my head a lot. The village of Garmish at the base of the Swiss Alps we stayed in looked like a scene from Hansel and Gretel. And there were Mercedes Benzes everywhere. Even the taxi cabs were Mercedes. That blew my mind.

Our tour bus driver, this cool German dude named Klaus, kept trying to get me to try the local food. Unfortunately, German food didn't agree with me too much. I didn't eat much while I was there and spent a lot of time in my room. No so for my band – they took in the sights and even took a gondola to the top of the Swiss Alps.

Armed Forces Entertainment's Elmo Gladden put together a great concert tour. They did spell my name wrong on the promotional posters but I didn't care. I still signed all of them. Our sound crew didn't speak any English at all, but they knew what they were doing and put together a stage and lighting setup for the troops that was second to none.

One cool thing about being in Germany was that I got to reconnect with my old childhood friend from Logan, Tommy Turner. I hadn't seen Tommy for over twenty years, but I knew he had been deployed to Germany. Once we were there, I asked someone from the military to try and find him. I was shocked when they told me they'd found Tommy and were setting up a reunion.

Tommy still looked the same. He walked in and we hugged and cried. He told me he and his unit were big fans of *America's Got Talent*. He said the show was carried on Armed Forces Television. He got all his buddies to vote for me. Still a bunch of them wouldn't believe we had grown up together. We solved that real quick and took more pictures than you can imagine. When it was time for dinner after the show, we had Tommy pile on the tour bus with us and come along. 5,000 miles away from home you can take the man out of West Virginia, but you can't take West Virginia out of the man. We had a ball!

After the shows, soldiers and their families would come up and thank me for performing. I was so humbled because it was me who should have been thanking them.

Team Landau Band

Ken Tackett	Drums
Brandon Willard	Drums/Percussion
Steve Hall	Drums
Dale Roberts	Guitar
Mark Smith	Keyboards
Duane Flesher	Piano
Sean Parsons	Piano
Jay Flippin	Piano
Bob Thompson	Piano
Steve Heffner	Bass
Greg Wing	Lead Trumpet
Kevin Moore	Trumpet
Martin Saunders	Trumpet
David Porter	Trumpet
Gordon Towell	Sax
Curtis Johnson	Sax
Marty Ojeda	Lead Sax
Ed Bingham	Sax
Matt James	Sax
Rick Tolbert	Trombone-1st
Joe Patton	Trombone-2nd
Mike Dotson	Trombone-2nd
Mike Stroeher	Trombone-3rd
Craig Burletic	Bass
Danny Cecil	Bass
Ernie Shaw	Bass Viola
Melissa Adams	Bass Viola

Also, Ernie Shaw and Melissa Adams—background vocals, John Griffiths, Ritchie Collins, Adam Whaley, Matt Stroge, and the whole team at Studimo, who make Landau sound great every night!

Chapter Twelve

Winning *America's Got Talent* hasn't been without its draw-backs. All the performers I met during the journey warned me to keep an eye on my business affairs. I was really concerned about blowing all the money before I even got started. I was so used to not having anything, I didn't want to make a wrong move. So even though we hired Kevin Dalton and Dwight Wiles from Smith Wiles and Co, a specialty firm in Nashville that handles a lot of entertainers – to watch over my business affairs, I became CEO of my own company, LEM Touring, Inc.

It's hard to keep up with all the business issues, but I sign all my own contracts and the company checks. Sometimes Kevin has to run me down in some hotel room to get my signature. That's okay by me. If it's coming in or going out, I make sure it has my signature on it. Burke, Jennifer and I are a good team here and I think my manager Burke is even tighter with my money than I am! He always gets the tiniest, cheapest rental car available—he's a big guy, and he has to fold himself up into them like he's in a clown car. He's always watching for good deals on airfares, too. We fly in and out of some weird airports and strange times to save some bucks. The dude really wants me to succeed long term. We always tell each other, it's a marathon, not a sprint.

I remember when I had to pay the first big check to the Internal Revenue Service. Burke came into the hotel room and explained the damages to me and then showed me the check I had to sign. It was the biggest check I had ever seen. It was also the biggest check he'd ever seen. I bet it took me 45 minutes to get up the courage to sign it. Every time I put the pen in my hand, I'd stop and put it back down. I just couldn't get used to the fact of giving that much money to the government. Burke kept saying, "Remember, if you weren't doing well, you wouldn't owe this much. This is a good thing." I wasn't buying it.

Finally, I looked at Burke. "What happens if I don't sign this check?" I asked.

He knew I was uncomfortable, but smiled, "Two words – Wesley Snipes," was all he said.

I signed the check.

We did a lot of shows in the first couple of months. Along with writing a big check to the government, I did splurge on a few things. We didn't have a car. My old boss Mike Ferrell had let us use a Toyota Camry off his lot for several months. Mike's the best. So, after things finally settled down for half a second, I called Mike and he set me up in a nice pre-owned SUV that was big enough to put my kids or my band in—a multi-purpose ride. And, since I wrecked Jennifer's car back when we first started dating, I also bought her a brand new Chrysler M-300. I needed to take care of my girl.

Truth is, I loved driving mine and Jennifer's new cars. It seemed like everywhere we went, we were getting picked up and chauffeured around in limos and staying in big suites. Tough life, right? But I missed driving and being a normal guy. At first all the traveling and staying in fancy hotel suites was fun. It was certainly different. At the Golden Nugget in Las Vegas, they put us up in a suite bigger than our old house back in Logan. The Greenbrier gave us an entire guest cottage. Every hotel suite was more over the top than the last one. They had hot tubs, conference rooms, full kitchens. They were massive. Remember, Jennifer and I had been living in my mother-in-law's guest room for the past several years. Every place we went Jennifer took pictures of the rooms, so she could show them to her mom.

Surprisingly though, what I discovered on the road was how much I actually enjoyed being back in Logan, especially when we bought our own home. Traveling was now part of a job. The more miles I logged, I could feel my roots pulling me stronger and stronger back to Logan. We had been living at Jennifer's mom's house since before our place had been broken into. The show had been over for nine months before we finally had time to find and buy a house. After some serious looking, we found the perfect house...not in Los Angeles, Nashville or New York...but back home in Logan. We loaded up our stuff and moved in. Since Miss Idella's house was overflowing with fan mail, awards and show merchandise, I think she was beginning to think her place was a Landau warehouse.

It's taken me a while, but I've really tried to read all the fan mail and respond when I can. Just like I try to stay around and meet folks after every show. I like to stick around and sign autographs and take pictures for all my fans. They've been good to me and I owe them everything. So, I'm usually the last person to leave the venue.

People say funny things to me in the autograph line. A lot of folks tell me they knew I was going to win from the first time they heard me. I always laugh when I hear that line. If somebody would've told me that at the time, it would've made the whole show a heckuva lot easier. The other thing people tell me that makes me laugh is they are glad I remained grounded and remain who I am. I find that funny, because who else could I be?

It can get weird, too. One night, I was sitting at a table signing autographs, when there's a big commotion behind me. I looked around and one of the guys in the band is pulling a pair of scissors out of some woman's hands. Apparently, this crazy lady was trying to cut off one of my dreads.

Along with the bizarre and hectic, it can be pretty cool at times. I met some of my heroes while out on tour. Boxer Sugar Ray Leonard and I appeared at a charity event together and I swear I think he could still go fifteen rounds. Larry King had me sing at his Friar's Club roast—his wife, Shawn Southwick, is a great singer in her own right. Donald Trump, Kathy Griffin, Don King, Judge Judy, Matt Lauer and Al Roker from the *Today Show*, Regis Philbin, and

Wanda Sykes were there along with a bunch of other celebs. And I met Dionne Warwick at an airport when we were playing gigs at competing casinos. Total class.

I've also had a few "shocks to the system" while on the road. One night I was performing in Chicago when an old girlfriend came up and told me I was her son's father. It had been a long time since I had seen her, but her son looked just like me (poor kid). Anyway, we got some blood tests done and Terrick is now the newest addition to our family. He comes to concerts whenever he can. When I had all my kids to our new house over Thanksgiving, he was there, too. He fit in great and his brothers and sisters took to him right away.

One of my biggest thrills was having my kids get to see me perform a split bill in Detroit at the DTE Energy Center with The Temptations.

I went to Detroit with some mixed emotions. I headed to the Motor City a few days early to spend some time with Terrick. Since I was there early, I also took the time to drive through my old neighborhood. Most of the houses were either abandoned or had been torn down. There was broken glass everywhere from street lights that had been shot out. A pack of wild dogs was roaming the street. The old house where I cut hair had about four feet of grass in the front lawn and boards in the windows. The entire block looked like a war zone.

The one thing that remained was the drug dealer who set up shop on the corner by my old house. He was still in business – the same guy.

If I went back to the 'hood with mixed emotions, I left confident the decision I made twenty years earlier to leave was the right one.

Later that afternoon I got to meet the great Otis Williams, founder of The Temptations. I had seen the movie about the Temps probably a hundred times and was psyched to get to meet Otis. They did their sound check first. Then, their band members hung out to listen to our sound check and complimented my guys on how tight they sounded. I invited Donnie Crosley (AKA "Don Q"), one of the guys I washed cars with back in Detroit, to come back-stage with me. He was blown away when the guys in The Temptations' band started asking me for an autograph.

Along with playing some great venues across America, I've also had the opportunity to be on some fun television and radio shows. The morning shows really throw you off schedule. When I performed on the *Today Show* in New York City, we had to be at the studio at 5:00 a.m. for a sound check. Then we had to sit around for a couple hours in the Green Room before actually performing.

Meeting Wendy Williams was fun because I am a big fan of her show. She is really tall. They had a Christmas set in the studio and I was singing "Baby It's Cold Outside" with Lara Johnston. She was not the person who sang with me on the album. That was Judith Hill from *The Voice*. But Lara sang background vocals for me at Caesar's Palace in Las Vegas and has a great voice. I found out later Lara's dad is Tom Johnston from the Doobie Brothers, so talent runs in the family. When we sang, they had this fake snow falling from the ceiling that kept dropping off my dreadlocks and into my mouth. I was just trying not to trip over the Christmas packages that were part of the set as we walked through singing. It you catch that clip on my website, you'll see what I'm talking about.

When we cut my album, Judith Hill and I recorded our vocals in the studio separately, on different days. So even though we had two "duets" on my album, we'd never actually met. The magic of showbiz, eh? We finally got to meet for the first time at the Hollywood Christmas Parade about an hour before we performed "Baby Its Cold Outside," for the telecast. Except it was sunny and 75° outside. It was nearly a disaster, because just before we got to the parade staging area, a wino kept following us and shouting at everyone in the crowd that he was the head of my record studio. Welcome to Hollywood!

I did the Piers Morgan show, but was disappointed when I found out Piers was actually on vacation. It was funny doing a show at CNN, because they were not used to having singers perform. They finally got the sound right with the help of John Deolp from Columbia, who came to the studio to help in the control room and it was a good show. It was also fun to be on *The View* with Barbara

Walters and Whoopi Goldberg, and *The Talk* in L.A. with Sharon Osbourne. I think she may have been my biggest supporter on the show.

One time I got to host a show on Sirius XM Radio called *Seriously Sinatra*. While I was in the Green Room waiting to go on, this tall skinny guy with long black hair walked in front of the door. It was Howard Stern. Someone told me Howard ripped me on his show. So I decided I wanted to meet him. Burke tried to stop me, but I headed out into the hall anyway and started shouting his name. He finally turned around and smiled. Rather than ripping me, he congratulated me on my victory. People were taking pictures and videos of us talking and we had a real nice discussion. The next day it was announced Howard Stern was replacing Piers Morgan as a judge on *America's Got Talent*.

What's Next

(because I don't want my book to have a Chapter 13)

When I won *America's Got Talent*, everybody in town expected I would pack up and leave Logan. They didn't know me very well. All my life I wanted to build my future in Logan. People see me pumping gas into my car and are surprised. "Why are you here?" they ask.

The answer is easy. Now that I have the financial resources to move from Logan, West Virginia, I'm not about to leave. I'm where I've always wanted to be. I'm home. In fact, Jennifer and I bought a house on the mountain where I used to tell my family I would build the town of Doonieville. Logan keeps me grounded.

It seems every place we play, people are wearing shirts announcing they are from West Virginia. It was really cool to be playing at the California State Fair in Sacramento and have a bunch of women in WV jerseys sitting in the front row.

I don't hide the fact I'm proud to be from West Virginia. It's been a real thrill to have met some of the great West Virginians. I got to meet Jerry West, one of the greatest to play in the NBA. And I played in a celebrity basketball game with NFL great Randy Moss. I hung out with Homer Hickam, author of the book *Rocket Boys*, which was made into the movie *October Sky* with Jake Gyllenhaal playing Homer.

On the music end, one night I got to sing for the induction ceremony at the West Virginia Music Hall of Fame. Butch Miles, Connie Smith and Kathy Mattea were there, as was Billy Cox (who played with Jimi Hendrix). Peter Marshall (from Hollywood Squares)– the Boy Singer – and filmmaker Morgan Spurlock were the hosts. I sat with Bill Withers ("Lean On Me, "Ain't No Sunshine, "Use Me" "Just The Two of Us, etc"). He kept telling jokes and cutting up. I think people were getting mad at us for laughing so much during the telecast. I couldn't help it. Withers was funny.

People ask me if all this has exceeded my wildest dreams and I tell them I dream pretty wild.

What are those dreams? Well let me tell you.

First, I'd like to take my music beyond my current audience. I play to a lot of white audiences. Don't get me wrong, I love all my fans. But black folks seem to forget that dudes like Sinatra and Martin invented cool. I'd like to think that the voice God has given me can help bridge that gap.

I envision a day when I release a dual CD – half crooner and half rhythm and blues—and we're selling it to young people. So much of today's music glorifies all that is bad and encourages them to go down an up and down path. I want kids to know the dreams I sing about from *The Great American Songbook*. I want my music to be a platform for positive.

When I listened to my dad playing in the basement, I didn't have to hear him sing. I bonded with the instruments. I could feel the soul and the music took me to another place. Jazz is global and I want kids to gain joy from it just like I did.

Secondly, I want to bring as much joy to my family, friends and fans as humanly possible. Jesus walked the Earth with a smile on his face greeting everybody. I admire Jesus more than anyone else (although I would love to have dinner with Michael Jordan). I enjoy every moment just to see what is going to happen next.

Finally, I want to see Doonieville become a reality. Oh, it may not be exactly what I envisioned as a kid. In fact, Doonieville may be here in Logan. Slowly but surely, I'll keep working to make the world a little better off than when I found it. And maybe, just maybe, you'll join me one day and be my guest at Doonieville.

Until then...Peace Out...y'all.

Love,
Landau

Acknowledgments

There are so many people who have helped me live out my dreams, it will be very hard to list them all. Still I'm going to try. I'm sure I'll miss someone, and for that I apologize.

First, and foremost, I want to thank God for making this all possible. Thanks to Him for giving me the strength and courage to pursue my dreams and to never give up. I truly believe He has a plan for each of us and I want to thank Him for never losing faith in me.

My family has meant everything to me throughout this journey. Mom and Dad both made sure that music was central in our house. Mom introduced me to Nat and Dad introduced me to funk. In hard times my grandparents, Flora Lee Page and Horatio Page, always made sure we had a roof over our heads and food on our table. They taught me great values and respect for my elders.

Thanks to my brothers and sisters—Pam Murphy (my first producer/manager), Anthony Page (for telling me to be myself), Alfonzo Murphy (for being my shadow as a kid), Melinda Murphy (for always being willing to step on a stage with me) and Shaun Simon.

Jennifer's mom, Miss Idella Monroe, and her late-husband, Wilbur "Jelly" Monroe, helped us a lot as a young couple. After Jelly passed, she let us live at her house and always had faith in my music.

When I was in Detroit, Pastor Haman Cross and his wife mentored me and kept me walking the straight and narrow. They saved my life.

I can't say enough about everyone at *America's Got Talent*— Thanks to Howie, Sharon, Piers and Nick for making me feel at home on their stage. Mike Farrell, Craig Brownstein and Denise Beaudoin all deserve a special shout out. Everyone at Freemantle Media and SYCO Entertainment…thanks for being there to help during the beginning of my television journey. Same things goes to everyone at Sony Music/Columbia Records who helped make my CD "That's Life" become a reality, and then a huge hit, especially Steve Tyrell, Jon Allen, Bill Schnee, John Doelp, Fran Defeo, Chris Poppe, Bob Mann, the incredible musicians on the album and all the folks at Wire Roads Studio in Houston Texas, and the famous Capitol Records studio "B" in Hollywood.

Team Landau has lots of moving parts and I appreciate all of them, like LA entertainment attorney extraordinare Roger Patton and Michigan attorney (and wanna be roadie) Aaron Cassell. Special thanks to Smith Wiles in Nashville- Dwight Wiles and Kevin Dalton are helping me hang onto what I've got. The same goes for my banker buddy Joe Raymond at BB&T.

The Landau Band is a great collection of fantastic musicians and vocalists. I've learned so much from them and am honored to share the stage with great performers including Ken Tackett, Brandon Willard, Steve Hall, Dale Roberts, Duane Flesher, Mark Smith, Sean Parsons, Jay Flippin, Bob Thompson, Steve Snyder, Ryan Kennedy, Steve Heffner, Greg Wing, Kevin Moore, Martin Saunders, David Porter, Gordon Towell, Curtis Johnson, Marty Ojeda, Ed Bingham, Matt James, Rick Tolbert, Joe Patton, Mike Stroeher, Mike Dotson, Ryan Kennedy, Craig Burletic, Danny Cecil, Ernie Shaw, Melissa Adams, Andre Williams and Misty Daniels. Special thanks to Jeff Flanagan for his hard work in putting together the original group of musicians.

Our production company Studimo is the first to show up and the last to leave at Landau shows. If we sound good, they're responsible…and if we don't, they're still responsible! They haul the heavy load from town to town, set it up and tear it down and we couldn't do what we do without the tireless efforts of John Griffiths, Ritchie Collins, Adam Whaley, Matt Stroge and the gang.

Thank you to a real legend in the music business Ken DiCamillo and his hard working associate Benjamin Schiffer at William Morris Endeavor, our booking agency. Also thanks to The Bazel Group (Ed and Gina), Lustig Talent (Richard, David and Cosetta) and

RMA (Rick, Chuck and Scott) for giving us the opportunity to perform for their clients. And to Jo Mignano and her team at Krupp Communications in New York and the Allen Media Strategies team in Washington D.C. for all the great P.R.!

Thanks so very much for the warm hospitality we always receive from Jim Justice, Jeff Bryant and Corey Worlick at the Greenbrier, our home-away-from-home. Legendary artist manager Peter Rudge (Peter helped manage The Who, The Rolling Stones, Lynyrd Skynyrd and Landau…now that's good company for me to be in!) and Mike Matsumoto, formerly of Octagon Entertainment, were a huge help in getting the ball rolling for Team Landau…thanks fellas.

Mike Ferrell at Mike Ferrell Toyota in Chapmanville, WV is one of the greatest bosses anyone could ever have. He always wanted me to succeed and gave me the freedom to pursue music. It was Mike who flew my whole family out to Hollywood for the final episode of *America's Got Talent*. Debrina Williams and all the folks at the Logan Chamber of Commerce gave me one of the first opportunities to showcase my talent in front of the whole town. Speaking of home town boys—a big shout out to Dave Allen and all the folks at WVOW for keeping me on the radio in Logan, to Jackie Tomblin and her team at the Coalfield Jamboree theatre and to Michael Lipton and the crew at the West Virginia Music Hall of Fame for their warm hospitality.

Thanks to the great artists I've had the honor to meet and share the stage with including Otis Williams and the legendary Temptations, the lovely and talented Kathy Mattea, Mountain Stage veterans Ron Sowell, Larry Groce and Michael Lipton, *American Idol's* Chase Likens, Judith Hill from *The Voice*, Lara Johnston, daughter of head Doobie Brother Tom Johnston and a terrific vocalist in her own right, the Davisson Brothers Band, Ms. Patti LaBelle, one of my all time heroes Bill Withers, filmmaker and music fan Morgan Spurlock, the hilarious Wendy Williams, Anderson Cooper, and the ladies from *The View* and *The Talk* TV shows.

Lots of folks have helped us out before and after my victory on *America's Got Talent*. Rick "Top Shelf" and Penny Lowe, Greg and Kim Wooten, Judge and Mrs. Eric O'Brien, Mitzi and Freddy Rick, Diana Barnette and her family, Governor and Mrs. Earl Ray Tomlin, Congressman Nick Rahall and Senator Joe Manchin are all great supporters of Team Landau.

I am proud that a West Virginian, Cathy Teets of Headline Books, is publishing my story. My award winning co-author Rick Robinson isn't a Mountaineer, but he did a good job at getting my story on paper just the same.

Two guys from Logan always have my back—my manager, Burke Allen, and my attorney and longtime pal, Bob Noone, are more than the top dawgs for Team Landau, they are my friends. Thanks, too, go to their wives, Cristi and Beth, who have let me "borrow" their husbands and take them away from home. I really appreciate you all.

My kids mean the world to me—Michael, Marcus, Kyra, Morgan and Terrick. I'm proud of every one of you.

My wife Jennifer always is and always will be "My Girl." She took me off the streets, changed my life and she has always loved me for who I am. She keeps me grounded. Thank you for sticking by me and for always having faith in me. I love you.

And to everyone who voted for me on *America's Got Talent*, came to a concert, watched me on television, waited in line for a picture or an autograph after a show, or just stopped me and said hello and to stay humble, your encouragement and kindness mean more than you'll ever know. Thank you for helping me to live my dream. God bless you!

About the Author

In November 2010, Landau Eugene Murphy, Jr. and his wife Jennifer left their hometown of Logan, WV for New York City, where they stood for over twelve hours outside the Jacob Javits Convention Center in Manhattan. They were among the thousands of people—young and old, singers, dancers, jugglers, mimes, and more — lined up to audition for NBC's *America's Got Talent*. It would take several more hours for Landau to finally get inside and sing a few bars, and his day grew even longer as he sang for one producer after another. Soon, he was the last one sitting in a huge rehearsal hall. "I knew that was a good sign," remembers Jennifer.

The rest as they say is history. After receiving standing ovations from judges Sharon Osbourne, Piers Morgan and Howie Mandel, singing a sizzling duet with the iconic Patti LaBelle, and crooning a rousing rendition of "My Way," Landau Eugene Murphy Jr. was named winner of *America's Got Talent's* sixth season on September 14, 2011. Just in time for Christmas 2011, Syco/Columbia Records released Landau's first album, "That's Life" and it debuted at number one on the Billboard jazz charts and the top 40 overall. Not only did his unique singing style make him stand out from all of his competition, Landau's humility, charm and confidence endeared him to the *America's Got Talent* judges, viewers, and audiences at his sold-out concert tour that launched in December 2011 and is still going strong.

Many have compared Landau's smooth vocals and phrasing to that of Frank Sinatra, a singer he's always admired. That's why many of the tracks from "That's Life" are Sinatra standards, but Landau does them his way. "I put my own voice and my own soul into this album," says Landau. "For many music fans, especially older people, I can bring back some happy memories. And hopefully, I can create new memories for generations to come. I think my album encompasses all of that. I want to give back as much as possible and stay true to the people who supported me."

Landau worked side by side with legendary record producer and Grammy Award winner, Steve Tyrell, himself an aficionado of Sinatra's music on "That's Life." During his storied 40-year music career, Tyrell has scored movies (That Thing You Do, Father of the Bride), produced albums for dozens of top artists (most recently, Rod Stewart's #1 album, Stardust: The Great American Songbook Volume III, Diana Ross, Ray Charles, Smokey Robinson, Linda Ronstadt, Mary J Blige, Chris Botti, Bonnie Raitt, Bette Midler and Stevie Wonder among them) and recorded his own albums.

"I loved working with Steve," says Landau. "He's so cool. We got along so well—he totally understood me and brought out the best in me." The vocals for the album were recorded in Houston and then in LA at the legendary Capitol studio "B" with a full orchestra on the same hallowed ground where Sinatra, Dean Martin, Judy Garland, Nat King Cole, and others have recorded so many classics. Tyrell and Landau have since performed together in New York, Los Angeles and Baltimore to audiences enthralled by the two vocal pros.

As part of his *America's Got Talent* prize, Landau realized a lifelong dream and headlined a show at the Colosseum Theater at Caesar's Palace in Las Vegas—the legendary playground for Sinatra and his iconic Rat Pack. Other tour stops include the Apollo Theatre, the DTE Energy Center in Detroit with Motown's Temptations, headlining appearances at the West Virginia and California State Fair, a Super Bowl appearance, a televised performance at The Hollywood Christmas Parade and a string of sold out headlining shows across the USA (many supporting local charities). Major media appearances have included *The Today Show, Anderson Cooper, The View, The Talk, The Wendy Williams Show, Fox and Friends, CNN, The Tom Joyner Show, Scott and Todd* on

WPLJ, *Good Day LA,* and many more. He's also honored his country by singing the National Anthem at Madison Square Garden, West Virginia University's Mountaineer Field, prior to a WVU/ LSU matchup and at several other public events.

"My father was a coal miner and he really loves music; my mother is from a musical family, too. After my parents split up when I was 8, I moved with my mother and two brothers and two sisters to Detroit," Landau explains. "It was completely different from Logan; I had to get used to the streets. My focus wasn't on school." He dropped out in the 11th grade to put his energy into looking out for the safety of himself and his family. "Church and basketball were the only things that got me out of the house and kept me going. I played for a church league, which kept me off the streets and they would take us to events where we could eat. Basketball was my first love and I grew up playing basketball with some great ballplayers like NBA star Chris Webber. There were times when I'd make a shot or dunk on someone and I'd run back down the court with a smile on my face singing 'Fly Me To The Moon,' everyone got a big kick out of it."

After moving back home to Logan in the late 1990's, Landau renewed a friendship with a childhood friend, Jennifer Carter. They started working together at a restaurant where she was a manager and they finally married in 2005. The proud husband and father of five says, "I love my kids and my wife with all my heart, more than anything, I want to make sure they don't have the same struggles I have. I want them to have more opportunities. I want them to be able to do what they want to do."

Despite going from washrags to riches, "I'm still happiest when I'm with my family," says Landau. "I like it when there is no stress and I'm doing what I want to do—which is to sing."

To find out the latest news on show updates, media appearances, fan opportunities and more, you can visit Landau Eugene Murphy Jr. online at www.landaumurphyjr.com. Fans can also follow Landau on his official Twitter page @landaueugenejr and his official Facebook page at www.facebook.com/landaueugenemurphyjr.com.

About the Co-Author

Rick Robinson is the award winning author of five novels and a columnist for several ezines including Tucker Carlson's, *The Daily Caller.* He is 2010 and 2013 Independent Author of the Year and 2011 International Independent Author of the Year with a win at the London Book Festival.

Rick's most recent novel, *Alligator Alley,* a departure from his previous four political thrillers, is a work of literary fiction about a man coming of age at age 50 set in the Florida Everglades. It was named Grand Prize Winner and Best Fiction at the Great Southwest Book Festival.

Writ of Mandamus was named Grand Prize Winner at the London Book Festival January 2012 and Rick Robinson carried off honors as International Independent Author of the Year. It was named Best Fiction at the Indie Book Awards.

Best selling author P.J. O'Rourke says that Rick Robinson "may be the only person on Earth who both understands the civics book chapter on 'How a Bill Becomes a Law' and knows how to get good seats at the Kentucky Derby."

Robinson's third novel, *Manifest Destiny*, was named 2010 Independent Book of the Year and he was awarded 2010 Independent Author of the Year. *Manifest Destiny* was also a Winner at the Paris and New York Book Festivals along with Finalist Awards in the USA News Best Book Awards for Best Thriller/Adventure, Best Fiction Indie Book Awards, Best Thriller Indie Excellence Book Awards, Best Thriller International Book Awards, and Honorable Mentions at the San Francisco, Hollywood, London, and Beach Book Festivals. This title has also been optioned by film producer, Peter Dyell, and is headed for the big screen in the future.

Rick's first book, *The Maximum Contribution*, and his second novel, *Sniper Bid*, both won major book awards.

Rick Robinson has thirty years experience in politics and law, including a stint on Capitol Hill as Legislative Director/Chief Counsel to then-Congressman Jim Bunning (R-KY). He has been active in all levels of politics, from advising candidates on the national level to walking door-to-door in city council races. He ran for the United States Congress in 1998.

Scrapbook

Memories

What People Say

Photos

Amazon Fan

"Ever since Landau first appeared on AGT, I've been anxiously awaiting his first album. Got my first copies today!! Yes, I certainly ordered more than just one! And, I'm so glad I did. At least now while I'm waiting for his second album, I'll be able to enjoy the first. If I wear one out, I've got plenty more to keep on listening.

First of all, I was never a Frank Sinatra fan. And I don't enjoy jazz. But, Landau brings this genre to new heights. His rendition is refreshing. His singing is so clean. And, he's making me wonder why I had never been a Frank Sinatra fan before. But, as far as I'm concerned, Landau takes Ole Blue Eyes' songs to a higher level of quality.

I highly recommend this album to anyone - even those who are not fans of jazz."

—DesertDeuces

A Tour is Born

Notes from the tour diary of manager
Burke Allen of Landau's first ever tour

December 3rd, 2011
Clay Center, Charleston, WV

    This show was Landau's very first concert appearance after winning AGT and the pent-up enthusiasm from his fans in his home state of West Virginia was incredible. They had put tickets on sale for this show and it literally crashed the computer system. There was a line of cars 6 blocks long outside the Clay Center of people trying to get into the box office to buy tickets. The venue sold out within 2 hours. When the time for the show came, Landau had a couple of performances with the big band that we had put together, made up of top musicians in the 4-state region around. Everyone wanted to play with Landau. There list of all the political and cultural dignitaries from the state were jockeying to try and get tickets. When it came time for Bob and I to introduce Landau before the show, the sound from the crowd when the spotlights were on them was deafening. It must have been like when the Beatles first came to America. There was loud, thunderous applause and cheering for Landau and a huge feeling of warmth and love, like the whole state was putting its arms around this guy. When he came on stage, they played the first note of the first song, "Ain't That a Kick in the Head," and the entire crowd rose to their feet. They gave him a long standing ovation before the show had even started. It was the most amazing, most incredible music thing I've ever seen, and I've seen a lot.

December 4th, 2011
Eastern KY Expo Center, Pikeville, KY

    As great as the first night was, the second night of the tour was snake-bitten. Emmy award winning tour pianist Jay Flippin didn't show up for sound check. Jay had driven himself to the show and wasn't answering his cell phone – we didn't know what happened to him. Jay had car trouble on the way to the show and his cell phone battery had died. The Eastern KY Expo center is an 8,000 seat venue; the sound and light crew had a difficult time adjusting from a theatre to a big cavernous room like that. Jay finally showed up 20 minutes before the lights went down, averting the major crisis of a "no piano concert." When Landau came out to sing, he started the first notes of his first song and had a microphone failure – they had to toss another mic to him. But none of that mattered because the crowd loved him and he was swarmed after the show by folks who wanted to pick up official Landau merchandise. Landau stayed and signed t-shirts and CDs for hours. That would go on to become the norm for every concert; we would always be the last ones to leave.

December 5th, 2011
Clay Center, Charleston, WV

Back to the Clay Center we went for a second sold out show. The good news was that they got their online computer ticketing back into shape, and tickets sold out in 39 minutes which still left a whole bunch more folks in Charleston who were unable to see Landau. As loud as the first night was, the second was even louder and more boisterous. What really struck me that night was that for the first time, I really had an appreciation for how fabulous the musicians were in Landau's band. It's very seldom that any artist today, because of the economics of travelling with such a large ensemble, performs with a full 18-piece big band. To hear all those horns and the full instrumentation really blows your hair back. These guys are as good as they come.

December 7th and 8th, 2011
Creative Arts Center, Morgantown, WV

Next was back to back shows in Morgantown, home to WVU (which had just been named the #1 party school in the nation by Playboy magazine – you can imagine that it was rowdy crowd). This was one of the first shows where we brought Landau out to walk through the crowd during the show. They had to hold up the show when a lady got so excited that she had fallen down and broken something and they had to call the paramedics. We started telling security to make sure that no one in the audience got hurt.

As Landau and I drove from the hotel to the Creative Arts Center (which was only a couple miles away), a huge snowstorm blew through. It was a complete whiteout and we couldn't find the CAC. We had a difficult time finding our own concert in the snow. On the brighter side, a local volunteer organization had a huge coat and glove drive for local children and we were very proud to be there and be a part of it.

December 16th and 17th, 2011
Smoot Performing Arts Center, Parkersburg, WV

The Smoot Performing Arts Center was run by a very dedicated community volunteer who was incredibly protective of "her" theatre. There were a few tense moments between the production crew and the theatre director at that show. It even ruffled Jennifer's feathers a bit, but in the end, Landau knocked it out of the park with two more sold out shows.

December 21st, 2011
Clay Center, Charleston, WV

We found ourselves back for a record breaking third sold out show at the Clay Center, which was the first time in the history of the theatre that had ever happened. The Clay Center management said they could have sold out another three performances; there just weren't enough days left before Christmas. That night, the autograph line after the show to meet Landau took several hours. We even offered to pay the security team extra to stay overtime to accommodate for it. We got back to the hotel around 3am.

December 22nd, 2011
Chuck Mathena Center, Princeton, WV

The Chuck Mathena Center was a beautiful new venue near the West Virginia border. Both of these shows sold out almost immediately because the venue holds less than 1,000 seats. We received major support on those tour dates from our friend Dreama Denver and her local *Little Buddy Radio* station. At the end of the second show, most of the band was on a tour bus headed, but we had chartered a small 4-passenger airplane to take Landau, Jennifer, myself, our production manager John Griffiths, and our band leader to the next city for some much deserved rest. Unfortunately, a major ice storm had blown in and Jennifer was a very nervous flyer. Because the plane was so small, Landau rode in the copilot seat. We were unable to fly out that evening because of the ice storm and we took off at dawn the following morning to get to our next concert outside of Pittsburgh. The weather hadn't improved much and Jennifer was especially incredibly nervous. Lots of prayers went up, but luckily, thanks to our pilot Alan and his great skill, we made it safely to the show.

December 23rd, 2011
The Harv at Mountaineer Casino near Pittsburgh, PA
     The Harv is part of the Mountaineer Casino and Racetrack Complex on the outskirts of Pittsburgh. It was bitterly cold at that show and we were all extraordinarily happy but anxious to get home to our families. After the ice storm fiasco, no one else would ride the plane home, so everyone piled onto the tour bus. Everyone except myself, who had decided to take a private ride home to the commercial airport in Leesburg, VA on the day of Christmas Eve. Unfortunately, it was not only bitterly cold but the heating mechanism in the private plane had malfunctioned, causing frost to form on the windshield the entire way back. The pilot and I were completely bundled up in coats and scarves as we flew into Virginia.

December 27th and 28th, 2011
Paramount Arts Center, Ashland, KY
     The Paramount Arts Center is a beautiful theatre in Ashland, KY, perhaps best known as the set of local hero Billy Ray Cyrus' *Achy Breaky Heart* video. Landau's show was on the 27th, two days after Christmas, and had sold out the first day it went on sale. We had also added a second show on the following day. At the end of the second concert, the Director of the Paramount Arts Center asked if we would consider adding a third show on two nights later. We were very, very nervous to do that with only 48 hours to get the word out about a third show, but ticket sales were as brisk as ever.

December 29th, 2011
Chuck Mathena Center, Princeton, WV

We headed back for a second show at Chuck Mathena Center, which had sold out a couple months before. There was a large group of veterans in the audience who were home for the holidays to spend time with their families and Landau took extra time to spend with them after the concert.

December 30th, 2011
Paramount Arts Center, Ashland, KY

We wondered if anyone would show up for the third Paramount Arts Center concert since the theatre only had 48 hours to promote the show. Amazingly, over 1,500 people in two days had purchased tickets for the third show there. It was a great way to cap off 2011!

Landau and Jennifer pose with a young fan during a CD signing at Budget Tapes and Records in Charleston, WV during a stop on Landau's first tour December 2011

Amazon Fan

I just saw Landau singing on the **Today Show** *and I couldnt believe my ears. The man's voice is the reincarnation of Frank Sinatra. I got on line to order his new CD and the price is so great I plan to order extra's for Christmas.*

Reading all the past reviews made me realize I'm not the only one who thinks this guy is special. After Googling him and finding out where he's come from, it makes you believe in the American Dream all over again.

—Big Fan in the desert

Media appearance list

Here's a short list of just some of the national media appearances that Landau has made, in addition to NBC TV's *America's Got Talent*

The Wendy Williams Show

The Anderson Cooper Show

The NAACP Image Awards (Landau nominated for Best New Artist in Hollywood, CA)

The International Reality Television Awards (Landau wins for Best Reality TV Personality in Hollywood, CA)

WVU vs. LSU football game on September 24th, 2011 - Landau performs the National Anthem on Mountaineer Sports Network

Marshall Thundering Herd basketball game – Landau performs the National Anthem on the Thundering Herd Network

Greenbrier PGA Classic golf tournament

The Today Show on NBC TV

The View

The Talk

The Tom Joyner Morning Show

Scott and Todd WPLJ New York/Dish Nation

Rob Shuter's *Naughty But Nice* on HDNet

Piers Morgan Tonight on CNN

The Daily Buzz syndicated TV

HLN's Showbiz Tonight

Entertainment Tonight

Access Hollywood

Extra!

The Hollywood Christmas Parade telecast on the Hallmark Channel

The Macy's Pittsburgh Christmas Parade telecast

SiriusXM's *Seriously Sinatra* channel

National Public Radio

Fox and Friends on the Fox News channel

Oklahoma City Thunder vs. Miami Heat basketball halftime show performance on the Thunder television network

West Virginia Lottery *Dream Big* statewide promotion with the WV State Fair

West Virginia Music Hall of Fame induction ceremony telecast on PBS

...plus hundreds of radio interviews, television appearances, newspaper and magazine interviews, and online articles.

Rare photos of Landau pre-dreadlocks

Landau Eugene Murphy Jr. performing in the May 2005 at the WE CAN Vaudeville show in Logan, WV—photo courtesy of Martha Sparks, Society Editor of The Logan Banner

Team Landau Gives Back

Here's a sample list of some of the charity events that we have been privileged to participate in.

Walking Miracles

Charity basketball game – 3rd Annual Kenneth "Honey" Rubenstein Juvenile Center

Coats for Kids drive with West Virginia Media Holdings

Appalachian Children's Chorus fundraising performance

The Houston Ballet fundraising gala at the Wertham Center in Houston, TX

Main Street Madison fundraiser

Habitat for Humanity celebrity basketball game

Charleston Montessori School fundraiser

Wheeling Youth Fundraiser at Capital Theatre

County-wide anti-bullying school assembly Webster County Schools charity fundraising appearance; in Webster County WV

WVU Mary Babb Randolph Cancer Research Center fundraiser

Denver Foundation fundraiser – Guinness Book of World Records for largest Gilligan's Island Theme Song Sing-Along

David Lee Cancer Center visit in Charleston, WV

Charleston Area Medical Center charity gala at the Clay Center

United Way Celebrity Waiter fundraiser at the Glade Springs Resort in Beckley, WV

Community Music Foundation Awards fundraiser at the Berry Hills Country Club in Charleston, WV

Remember the Miners Golf Tournament in Beckley, WV

We Can! Vaudeville show special appearance

Dell Webb retirement performances in Hilton Head, SC

Children's Home Society Independent Grocers fundraiser

Golden Girls Group Home fundraising performance at the Keith Albee Theatre in Huntington, WV

Statesville High School band fundraising performance in Statesville, NC

County-wide anti-bullying school assembly at the Logan Memorial field house

Walking Miracles Cancer Survivors Dinner with Sugar Ray Leonard

WVU Athletic Scholarship Fundraiser Dinner and Fashion Show

Aracoma Story outdoor theatre appearance to introduce *Ring of Fire*

Surprise Valley Children's Summer Camp appearance in Beckley, WV

Tamarack Foundation fundraising dinner and appearance

Highland Hospital foundation fundraising dinner performance

West Virginia Freedom Festival Veteran's Recognition ceremony

Southern Leadership Conference performance in Charleston, WV

West Virginia Coal Association performance

Girls Night Out fundraising appearance for the YWCA RESOLVE's Hope House at the Sunrise Mansion in Charleston, WV

West Virginia Blazers celebrity basketball fundraising game in Wyoming county, West Virginia

West Virginia Hospital Association Gala fundraiser performance

Grady Health Foundation benefit in Atlanta, GA

Armed Forces Entertainment performances for US troops stationed in Germany

CASA (Court Appointed Special Advocates) of West Virginia Christmas concert in Ripley, WV

Cans for Christmas food drive for the Salvation Army at the Raleigh Playhouse Theatre in Beckley, WV

Cans for Christmas food drive for the Salvation Army at the Coalfield Jamboree in Logan, WV

Southern West Virginia Women's Expo in Beckley, WV

Veteran's Hospital Women's Center building grand opening in
 Huntington, WV
Junior Achievement of West Virginia benefit concert at the
 Charleston Municipal Auditorium
Charity basketball, National Anthem performance and player
 appearance in Logan, WV
The Hatfield McCoy Trail Days charity ride and appearance in
 southern WV
Southern West Virginia Community and Technical College
Applied Technology campus building dedication and ribbon
 cutting with Governor Tomblin in Williamson, WV
Daymark of West Virginia charity gala at the Executive Air
 Terminal in Charleston, WV
Logan County Chamber of Commerce annual fundraising
 dinner performance in Logan, WV
Town of Middlebourne 200th Birthday Celebration
West Virginia Power Park Celebrity Challenge baseball game
 for the Charleston Montessori School in Charleston, WV
The Everest Institute Community Day for the March of Dimes
 in Cross Lanes, WV
Milan Puskar fundraiser at the Waterfront Place Hotel in
 Morgantown, WV

Landau's Christmas CD

Landau's love of family, his West Virginia home and his responsiveness to those 14 million weekly viewers who helped vote him into the top spot on AGT by the biggest margin in the top rated TV show's history. "Everywhere I've gone in the past two years, people keep asking me if I'd do a Christmas album. I love holiday music, and I'm happy to give folks what they want," says the soft-spoken crooner of his second album *Christmas Made For Two*.

The album, recorded in West Virginia with producer/engineer Ritch Collins and audio mastering by Jeff Bosley features Landau's trademark rich vocal textures backed by an all-star lineup of musicians (including several members of Murphy's touring band). Highlights include up-tempo, horn driven takes of "White Christmas" and "Santa Claus Is Coming To Town" along with romantic fireplace and mistletoe ballads like "The Christmas Song (Chestnuts Roasting On An Open Fire)" and "I'll Be Home For Christmas."

Fresh, jazzy spins on "Let It Snow" and "I've Got My Love To Keep Me Warm" blend perfectly with holiday originals including "Quiet Christmas" by jazz piano great Bob Thompson and the title track "Christmas Made For Two" from veteran Nashville songsmiths Jeff Peabody and Scott Krippayne. A heartfelt duet featuring Landau and former Temptations lead vocalist Glenn Leonard on a spiritual, understated "Silent Night" round out the album. Leonard reprises his lead vocal on the classic from the smash hit "Temptations Christmas" album, which is heard on radio stations around the world every holiday season. "I'm a huge Temptations fan, so what a blessing to be able to share the studio with Glenn, and learn from him about how the Temptations made their Christmas album so timeless," said Landau. We have a feeling that Murphy's own *Christmas Made For Two* is sure to be in perennial heavy rotation around many a Christmas tree for many years to come.

What People Say

Here's what some friends, fans, and band members had to say about Landau

Landau Eugene Murphy Jr. is a true Champion For Children. Although having been faced with many difficulties in his own life, Landau's passion and concern for those less fortunate is what makes him special to so many. For many years the work of the Children's Home Society has benefited greatly because Landau carries the stories of our children in his heart, and in his words by encouraging others to help West Virginia's children. Landau inspires us all because he truly believes that everyone can do something to help children.

For many years the Children's Home Society's Volunteer program in Logan has held a fundraising event called "Vaudeville." This is how we came to know our Landau. Landau would perform with Bob Noone at the event. Each year Landau would come back and sing tirelessly to help Children's Home Society raise money to meet the needs of children in Logan and surrounding Counties. Everyone was amazed at this tall, skinny, young man, whose giant and amazing voice, made us smile, made us cry, and made us "want to sing".

— Mary White Chief Operations Officer, Children's Home Society of West Virginia

The band was on the way out to Arizona and due to a layover, we all went to grab a late dinner. As we were sitting there, a young man who was in his army uniform passed by the table. It was at this point that Landau quietly put out his hand and said, "Thanks for your service." It wasn't a public display, but rather a private and sincere gesture of gratitude. This wasn't an isolated case; I saw, time and time again, his hand reach out to service men and women every time he came in contact with them. It was always private, and always sincere.

— Sean Parsons, pianist and arranger for the Landau Eugene Murphy Jr. Orchestra and music instructor at Ohio University, Athens, OH

As an agent, I spend time watching the various music competitions. When I first saw Landau, I was obviously rooting him on as a fellow Mountaineer. However, when he opened his mouth and sang, it was something both unexpected and amazing. I knew the guy had not only talent but mega talent.

While I never met him or knew little about him, I was very proud that he won *America's Got Talent* and hoped that we would have the opportunity to work with him at some point

Since then, we have had several opportunities to work with Landau and his folks. All I can say is it has been a wonderful experience.

The first time I worked with him, he pulled into the venue in his bright white SUV and parked. He got out and then more folks got out, and then more folks got out... He was carrying the whole family – it was great! Throughout the day, it was obvious that everyone had a part in the show. It was a team effort and he shared the spotlight with everyone.

Another important observation about Landau is that he allows others the opportunity to be showcased. On more than one occasion, he has had a young performer with him and gave them time on stage to perform and showcase their talents. It is impressive to see him helping young talent to find their way on to the stage and begin chasing their own dreams.

We have been blessed with the opportunity to work with Landau, his family and Team Landau. It has been a great experience. I admire him for what he has accomplished. I am impressed that he is a humble person... someone who knows who he is, where he is from, and gives so much back to our state and his fans. He is a great ambassador for West Virginia and the music industry. He is great to be around and is truly a nice guy with a great sense of humor and quick wit. His story is amazing, and can be an inspiration to others.

— Rick Modesitt, President of Rick Modesitt & Associates, Inc., national talent booking agency

I didn't watch *America's Got Talent* and I didn't care to. I would hear folks talking about a guy from West Virginia who was on the show and how good he was. My interest was peaked a bit, but not enough to actually tune in to the show (the West Virginia people never win). A few weeks later the subject came up again; a guy from Logan, WV, who works at a car wash, is still on AGT. As a matter of fact, it was a post on Facebook. So, I clicked the link. WOW, Landau Eugene Murphy Jr. is awesome!

I decided to tune in to the next episode. Again, I was amazed. However, people from West Virginia just never win—anything.

I continued to watch over the next few weeks to see how far Landau would get. I enjoyed Silhouettes, was proud for POPLYFE and was amazed at Team iLuminate. However, there's a guy from West Virginia on this show who can wail it. Let's go Landau!

Over the next couple weeks I watched with great anticipation. Finally, "the winner is... Landau Eugene Murphy Jr.!" I was quite excited. I was proud. I was humbled.

But then! I get a call from my great friend Burke Allen. Burke was my first boss when I entered the world of broadcast radio and je continued to mentor me throughout my early years in radio. I had kept in touch with Burke over the years as he roamed the country pursuing his passions of entertaining people.

So, Burke goes on to explain that he is now Landau's manager and needed a little assistance with a Charleston, WV event in which the 2011 winner of *America's Got Talent* would be featured.

Over the next few days I had the opportunity to get to know Landau and his wife, Jennifer. They are amazing people – tender-hearted, humble, southern West Virginia folks. I recall a meet and greet at Budget Tapes and Records in Charleston where folks lined up around the building to get a picture and autograph. Landau never tired. At least he never showed it. During this event, I remember watching Landau and Jennifer share tears with a lady who shared with them a touching story. Amazing people.

Fast forward to June 2012. I am a director for Surprise Valley Youth Camp — a Christian youth camp in Beckley, WV. I knew Landau would be in the area for an event at Tamarack. I called Burke and asked if it would be possible for Landau to make an appearance for the children attending the camp.

Burke made it happen. Not only did Landau come for a visit, but his wife came along as well. Landau spoke to us and explained that it is OK to have dreams and to follow them. After that, he joined us in a couple verses of Amazing Grace.

Before leaving, Landau and Jennifer stood for a couple hours, signing autographs and posing for pictures for over 100 campers and staff. This was a surprising and exciting time for all. Again, the Murphy's kept smiling and refused to show that they were exhausted (and had the right to be).

I must continue to say thank you to Landau, Jennifer and Burke Allen with Allen Media Strategies.

Thanks for Dreaming Big!

— Scott Pauley, Minister of Stewart Park Church of Christ, Cross Lanes, WV

Landau is a very special person to me. He is my friend and my mentor and he has allowed me to fulfill the dreams that I've had since I was a child. I really enjoy being a part of Team Landau and I hope I can always be a part of his team 'til the end. Congratulations Doon-Doon on your success!

— Melissa Adams, touring background vocalist

Since I began working with him, Landau has continued to have a profound positive effect and inspiration to me. As a performer, he continues to grow and wow the crowds. As a person, he is as genuine and giving as they come. I have a friend for life in Landau.

— Dale K. Roberts, lead guitarist, Landau Eugene Murphy Jr. Big Band

Landau with the Director of the Hatfield-McCoy Convention and Visitor's Bureau and Executive Director of the Logan County Chamber of Commerce Debrina Williams

I did an arrangement that we performed together of Beethoven's "Joyful Joyful" morphing into Curtis Mayfield's Civil Rights anthem "People Get Ready" at First Presbyterian Church of Anniston, AL in 2010. What a great memory! – Bob Noone, Landau's friend and attorney

I have had the pleasure of booking Landau for several events at The Greenbrier Resort. I recall one event where I drove down to his cabin to take him to a meet and greet. He came outside on the porch and we both waited for his wife Jennifer and manager Burke to get ready. As we stood there, I wasn't sure what was going on. He didn't say anything. I can tell he didn't want to talk, so I didn't force any conversation. He seemed very sad and depressed. I couldn't help but to think, how can this guy feel this way. He won a million dollars using the talents that God gave him, he has the world at his finger tips, travels the world, and gets paid to do it. What was wrong? Many times at other events, he had seemed almost playful like a big kid. Not today.

Jennifer and Burke came out and we drove to the private meet and greet event. Landau posed and smiled with the private party guest, as if everything were great. He still didn't engage in too much conversation, but he gave the fans what they asked for. Later on that evening, he would perform for this private group. He did a fantastic job!!! It was a very special show; one of my favorite performances by him ever. He surprised me when he told everyone in the room that he was sad. His grandmother had passed away today and he wanted to dedicate this song to her. It was Donny Hathaway's "A Song For You." This was out of the ordinary to hear him perform in an almost street credit genre. This was straight from the heart, hardcore, it was 100% pure R&B. Being known for singing Frank Sinatra was one thing, but to sing something from the complete other end of the spectrum, and do it well, revealed that Landau had more than a great voice. He has deep emotion and soul tied into his performance. He brought tears to the audience. There was so much passion and dedication in his voice. I recently lost my grandmother at age 90, and I reflected back to watching Landau express his love for losing his grandmother. All I can say is thank you Landau, watching you put your all into that performance helped me through my loss as well. Thank you for "A Song For You" …for me.

— Corey Warlick, manager of music and entertainment at the Greenbrier Resort

As Society Editor of The Logan Banner, I attend a lot of functions, especially those events that are fundraisers for local causes. Every May, the local West Virginia Children's Home Society WE CAN (Working to Eliminate Child Abuse and Neglect) holds their annual WE CAN Vaudeville Show. I had been attending them since I assumed my position in 2001. Always entertaining, there never were any astounding moments. That is until Landau walked on stage in May 2005. The audience gave him a typical greeting with their applause as they did other performers.

Then the music started and he began to sing… within minutes the audience was on their feet clapping, giving their catcall whistles and cheering him on. Never in the previous years had I witnessed such a reception to one of the performers. The expression on the faces in the audience back in May 2005 was the same expression I saw on the judges when I watched him do his first audition on *American's Got Talent.*

Landau won the hearts of Logan County back in May 2005 in his first appearance at the WE CAN Vaudeville Show and their appreciation of his talent carried through to his competition on *America's Got Talent.* During his competition, people from across the country would call The Logan Banner newsroom with questions about Landau. Many wanted to know if he was as he appeared on television. My answer was, "Yes, that is Landau."

It is also refreshing to know that his "fame" has not changed him; he is still the same Landau I met more than eight years ago.

— Martha Sparks, Society Editor of *The Logan Banner*

During a rare day off during his Spring 2012 tour, Landau did three presentations to our schools. We bused all the students in to see him at our local field house. What an inspiration Landau is to students with his positive message of never giving up and dreaming big!

—Wilma Zigmond, former superintendent, Logan County
Board of Education

The first time I saw Landau was of course on his appearance on *America's Got Talent*. Like the judges and the studio audience and all of America, I expected him to just belt out some R&B, and instead he nails a Frank Sinatra tune. He impressed all of America and impressed them so much that he went on to win.

As a talent agent for Landau, he's always made our firm look like the hero. Every buyer has said the same thing: that the show was phenomenal and that Landau is extremely easy to work with.

Also, as a person who has seen Landau perform live, I'm very impressed with him and his short period of exposure to the entertainment world. He's already learned how to read his crowd and adapt to the show accordingly. One night, I saw that his performance wasn't exactly hitting the crowd. Landau immediately switched to something else and had them "eating out of the palm of his hand."

Landau is a great performer and a great guy. I look forward to his continued success.

— Richard Lustig, President of Lustig Talent, Orlando, FL

An emotional moment during the Welcome Home Celebration just after winning America's Got Talent

I heard him before I saw him. It was the style of music that first caught my attention. The voice I heard was crooning the music of Frank Sinatra; not the usual fare in a small town talent contest. Delighted and curious, I walked toward the stage, drawn to that voice.

To my surprise there stood a smiling, tall and skinny black man, sporting a little derby hat. The audience was enthralled with his performance. Landau Eugene Murphy, Jr. took first place that evening during the local festival.

In pursuing his dream, he has inspired others to gather their courage and dare to pursue their own. To phrase it in his words, Dream Big! After all, he is proof that dreams can come true!

What is most amazing about this unique young man is that he continues the journey, doing what he loves to do, singing his style of music and meeting people!

— Debrina Williams, Director of the Hatfield-McCoy Convention and Visitor's Bureau and Executive Director of the Logan County Chamber of Commerce in Logan, WV

I'll never forget playing with Landau at his very first show at the Clay Center in Charleston, WV. I love playing with Landau because the music and arrangements are always extremely well written and Landau absolutely captivates his audiences.

— Greg Wing, lead trumpet and professor of music/trumped at Morehead State University

My favorite show of Landau's, by far, was the Gilligan's Island themed show in Bluefield, WW. Landau has incredible musicianship and he always 'brings it' to every single performance.

— Gordon Towell, saxophone and professor of jazz at
Morehead State University

From a player's perspective, playing with the Landau band is tremendous, but that goes hand-in-hand with the affable personalities of Jennifer and Landau. They are wonderful people.

My most memorable show has to be Clarksburg, WV. Fifteen minutes before show time, a major rainstorm blew into the outdoor amphitheater we were set to perform in. As the production crew scrambled to cover the stage, instruments, and equipment, the band huddled in the small backstage dressing room to wait out the storm. The crowd of over 2,000 headed out of the amphitheater to wait in their cars and listen to the radio for word of whether the concert would be cancelled. The rain kept coming; we kept waiting. The local TV meteorologist was the emcee for the show and was checking in with the TV station and their Doppler radar to watch for a break in the storm. At about 11:15, three and a half hours after the show was supposed to start, the monsoon finally ended. The gear was uncovered and the concert went on. To our amazement, most of the crowd had waited in their cars the entire three and half hours and came back into the concert.

On a much sunnier note, we headlined the main stage in the Sunshine State of California at the State Fair in Sacramento. I lived in the Nor Cal for 22 years, playing professionally. I was instrumental (ha!) in getting eight players from that area that are good friends, amazing players, and wonderful people to play with Landau.
— Rick Tolbert, lead trombone

I have always appreciated the high level of musicianship and camaraderie that comes with the experience of playing with Landau.
— Michael Stroeher, trombone for the Landau band, professor of trombone at Marshall University, and Principal Trombone for the Huntington Symphony Orchestra

I love getting to play with the seasoned vets in Landau's band. We keep great music alive by DOING it LIVE! A few of my favorites gigs that I've played with Landau include the first show in our hometown of Logan, WV: the city where my parents met. We also played on the Creative Arts Center stage at WVU in the building where I met my wife. And I'll never forget the show where we played to thousands of soaking wet, but enthusiastic fans.

— Marty Ojeda, lead saxophone with the Landau band, and band director at Logan High School

The most memorable trip that I've taken with Landau was our trip to Germany. We got to pay for our troops and their families who were stationed there.

As a veteran myself, my most memorable trip that I've taken with Landau was our trip to Germany. We got to pay for our troops and their families who were stationed there. We were met with very enthusiastic crowds of soldiers and their families all across Germany. It was fun to see Landau try the local cuisine.. I'd never thought I'd hear the words, "Landau Murphy" and "wienerschnitzel" in the same sentence! In addition to the great music and watching his rapport with his audience during a show, I enjoy knowing Landau personally and knowing that he is the same person offstage that he is onstage. With Landau, "what you see is what you get!"

— Duane Flesher, tour pianist, and pianist with the Smoot Theatre House Band

Playing our first gig in Charleston was unforgettable – the thousands of fans there were electric! I always love hanging out with Landau before a gig. He's a genuine guy who is kind and FUNNY!

— Curtis E. Johnson, saxophone with the Landau band

Our first performances at the Clay Center in Charleston were GREAT! Playing sold out shows to throngs of Landau fans was an experience I'll never forget. Not only is Landau a great entertainer, but the band is made up of the region's finest musicians. It's been great getting to know and play with them all.

— Matt James, saxophone with the Landau band, and Professor of Saxophone and Jazz Studies at Ohio University, Athens, OH

After playing a huge 2,000-seat show in Orlando the night before, the tour was booked into a very prestigious but small jazz club right on Cocoa Beach in Florida. Both of the evening shows were sold out and the club was packed. It must have been 100 degrees on the stage under the lights, but Landau gave it everything he had and turned in two incredible performances. I love hearing stories about Landau growing up in Detroit and how he made it on *America's Got Talent.*

— James Steven Hall, touring drummer and percussionist, and Coordinator of Percussion Studies at Marshall University

Billboard posted during airing of America's Got Talent

As the youngest guy in the Landau band, I'm used to getting jazzed (HA!) by the other members. Landau likes to say that I look like Shaggy from Scooby-Doo in concert. The truth is, there no one else I'd rather play my bass behind. Landau is the best!

I also got to fulfill my lifelong dream of visiting Germany during my tour with Landau there – something I'll never forget.

— Steven Heffner, upright and electric bass guitar

My two favorite things in the world, outside being with my family, are playing golf and playing drums with the Landau band. I'm honestly not sure which one is more fun. Landau is easy to work with, has incredible stage presence and vocal skills, but most of all, has a huge heart. It's my honor to drive the bus for Team Landau.

— Ken Tackett, drummer for Team Landau and head of the West Virginia Golf Association

I'll never forget our trip to play in Germany for our Armed Forces Entertainment. Our first tour stop was in the village of Garmish, performing for the military at the base of the Alps. It looked like a little Bavarian gingerbread Christmas town. Landau has such a highly entertaining personality and the caliber of musicians that are in the band is outstanding. They're people that can play music, not just notes. They put a lot of soul in it. And we have always have fun together!

— Mark Smith, keyboards and synth with the Landau band, and music instructor at Marshall University

Playing with Landau is a gas! I'm the tour percussionist, which means that I play all the odd little noisemakers like conga drums, xylophone, tympani, and even sleigh bells during the Christmas shows; I've got a lot going on. Sometimes, I still just stand back and watch Landau perform. What an incredible entertainer!

— Brandon Willard, tour percussionist

Somewhere in Kentucky on Country Music Highway

During our first Christmas tour, the Director of the Smoot Theatre in Parkersburg released a blizzard of fake snow onto the stage and surprised everyone, especially Landau. Snow was coming down on him and into his dreads, and without missing a beat, Landau looked into the audience and said, "Ladies and gentlemen, tonight it looks like I've got Dread and Shoulders." That might just be the funniest line I've ever heard in a concert.

There's a general sense of community and ownership in the concert experience we all put out for Landau's fans. It's so nice to be there with the guys when everybody cares about the product; no body looks at it like it's just another job. Everybody seems to be proud of the moment that we're creating onstage. I've been around many, many entertainers and with Landau, what's evident to me is that he really cares about people. He cares about the people he works with and he cares about the people in the audience. Once he was exhausted after a show, and he signed some CDs for my kids, who had both gone through bone marrow transplants. He told them to stay strong and he put an arm around them without really even knowing them. That sense of genuine quality about his character shows that he has a great empathy for people.

— Martin Saunders, trumpet with the Landau band and instructor at Marshall University

I was presenting the "Sinatra of Soul" to Alabama fans, under my theory that you "have to have a place to be bad before you have a place to be good." Strange thing was, Landau was never BAD! – Attorney and friend Bob Noone

Photo courtesy of Charleston Daily Mail

"I am proud to say that Landau is from my hometown of Logan, West Virginia – a small town, to be sure, but a tight-knit one. I know many Logan folks have been inspired by his success and, most important, I believe they appreciate that he continues to be the down-to-earth, friendly next-door neighbor Logan has always known Landau to be. I wish him the best of luck at all his future endeavors, though I know he won't need it – Landau has that combination of hardworking spirit and one-in-a-million talent that has gotten and will get him where he wants to go. He is a true West Virginian and I'm proud of him."

—Governor Earl Ray Tomblin

With Sugar Ray &
Archie Talley

With Vegas legend
Clint Holmes

130

With comedian Capone backstage
at the Apollo

Landau and his band perform with Davisson
Brothers Band at the request of the
Governor at PGA's Greenbrier Classic

Clarksburg with fans

Speaking to school kids with sports star Pat White

Today Show Set!

TODAY

What a very talented person, and so glad that someone that wins on America's Got Talent that you hear about again. If you like the old style of singing then you need to listen to this man. He is very good. His singing will take you back to the Rat Pack area.
—Amazon Reviewer,
Lafayette, New York

With NY Giants
co-owner
and Hollywood
producer
Steve Tisch

With co-author
Rick Robinson

With Kathy Mattea

With actor
Boris Kodjoe

Jet Ride en route
to WVU vs. LSU

Before shooting hoops at a charity basketball game with NFL star Randy Moss, Pat White, and other WVU greats

In studio with Glenn Leonard, former lead singer of The Temptations

Landau and his producer
Steve Tyrell

On the sidelines with
former NY Giants running
back Ahmad Bradshaw

Receiving the West Virginia Governor's Arts "Artist of the Year" Award from West Virginia Governor Earl Ray Tomblin

Singing the National Anthem at West Virginia Governor Earl Ray Tomblin's Inauguration

With manager Burke Allen before performing at the CA State Fair

Appearing on NBC TV in Maryland with a fan and Olympic torch runner

144

At Book Expo America in New York City with Miss Northern WV's Outstanding Teen—Krystian Leonard

With Miss West Virginia USA 2012—Andrea Rogers

On stage during AGT Live; one of
three sold-out shows in a row at
Caesar's Palace in Vegas

Showing love for the
Marshall Thundering
Herd on stage with the
Huntington Symphony
Orchestra

competing for a million dollars on
America's Got Talent!

Lunching in Beverly Hills while discussing new CD with music producer Jeff Weber and manager Burke Allen

On set with the team from The Daily Buzz TV show

Doing the West Virginia Mambo with kids
during the music video shoot

149

Landau and Liza
Minnelli's musical
director Billy Stritch

Landau on stage with guitarist
Dale Roberts at the Hospice Fundraiser

ARMED
FORCES
ENTERTAINMENT

With manager Burke Allen
at the Apollo

His CD (That's Life) will
make you smile! Landau was
wonderful in concert and the
CD brings the experience back
every time I hear it.
—Amazon Reviewer, Niceville, FL

With Mark Kennedy Shriver

On the red carpet with
Larry and Shawn King

151

What a voice! What a guy! What a album!! Landau can sing anything! I am so glad I was blessed to see his career take off and order this album before it even came out
—Amazon Reviewer, Oklahoma

152

At The Apollo with friend
and singer Chris Curry

Waiting out a rain delay with percussionist Brandon Willard

Listen folks I am a country and bluegrass kind of guy NOT into this type of music!!!!! However I heard this guy on TV and I had to order it. Great music UNREAL voice!!!

Highly recommend.
—Amazon Reviewer,

"I don't want to ever forget where I came from." - Landau

In the studio

Landau is my hero. This is a great CD. I love it! His voice conveys so much depth and soul. It makes these old hits somehow new. GREAT CD!
—Amazon Reviewer, Gibbon, MN